94

9

MISSOURI
Then and Now

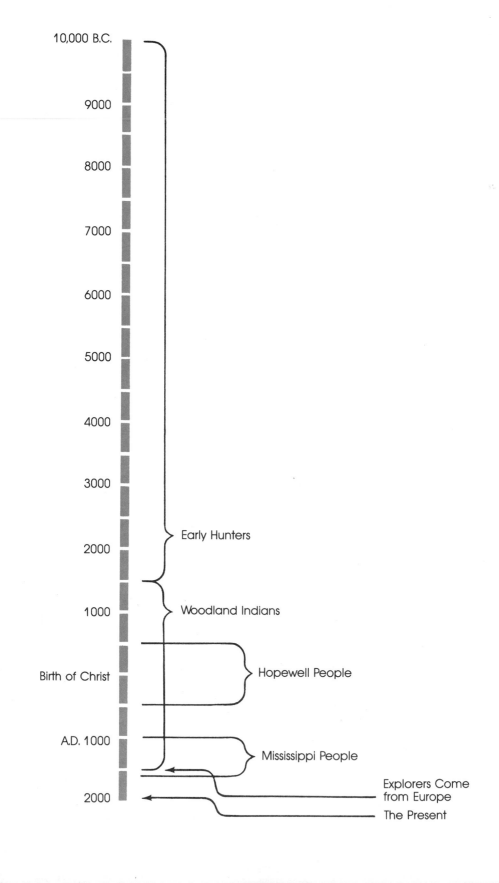

10,000 B.C.

9000

8000

7000

6000

5000

4000

3000

2000

Early Hunters

1000

Woodland Indians

Birth of Christ

Hopewell People

A.D. 1000

Mississippi People

Explorers Come
from Europe

2000

The Present

MISSOURI
Then and Now

Revised Edition

Perry McCandless and
William E. Foley

University of Missouri Press
Columbia and London

Library of Congress Cataloging-in-Publication Data

McCandless, Perry, 1917–
    Missouri then and now / Perry McCandless and William E. Foley. —
Rev. ed.
        p.   cm.
    Includes bibliographical references and index.
    Summary: The history and development of Missouri are traced in
this textbook which includes illustrations, suggested activities,
and glossary.
    ISBN 0-8262-0825-8 (alk. paper)
    1. Missouri—Juvenile literature.   [1. Missouri.]   I. Foley,
William E., 1938–.   II. Title.
F466.3.M32   1992
977.8—dc20   91-42325
                                                                          CIP
                                                                          AC

∞™ This paper meets the requirements of the
American National Standard for Permanence of Paper
for Printed Library Materials, Z39.48, 1984.

Designer: Kristie Lee
Typesetter: The Composing Room of Michigan, Inc.
Printer and Binder: Walsworth Publishing Company
Typefaces: Avante Garde, Palatino

Contents

Chapter 1   The First Missourians   1

Chapter 2   A Rich Land   19

Chapter 3   Europe Discovers America and Missouri   36

Chapter 4   Life in French Missouri   52

Chapter 5   Missouri Becomes a Part of the United States   69

Chapter 6   Life on the Frontier   89

Chapter 7   Early Travel   104

Chapter 8   Missouri and the West   116

Chapter 9   A Growing State   133

Chapter 10   A Divided Country   147

Chapter 11   The Civil War Comes to Missouri   161

Chapter 12   Reconstruction in Missouri   176

Chapter 13   Changing Times in Missouri   187

Chapter 14   Good Times and Bad Times   207

Chapter 15   Missourians in the Modern World   225

Chapter 16   Government in Missouri   243

Chapter 17   Missouri Today   254

Chapter 18   Fine Arts in Missouri   269

Appendix   State Symbols   283

Acknowledgments   287

Glossary   289

Index   299

Famous Missourians

Big Soldier: Osage Indian Leader   14

Auguste Chouteau: French Trader and Businessman   46

Jeanette Fourchet: Free Black Pioneer   56

Meriwether Lewis and William Clark: American Explorers   76

Mary Easton Sibley: Pioneer Settler   82

Saint Rose Philippine Duchesne: Frontier Missionary and Teacher   96

Samuel L. Clemens: Writer   108

James P. Beckwourth: Mountain Man   120

George Caleb Bingham: Frontier Artist   140

John Berry Meachum: St. Louis Businessman and Preacher   154

Francis P. Blair, Jr.: Politician and Soldier   162

James Milton Turner: Educator and Diplomat   180

Susan Elizabeth Blow: Teacher   196

John J. Pershing: Soldier   210

Harry S. Truman: American President   232

Lucile H. Bluford: Journalist and Civil
Rights Leader   236

Stuart Symington: Politician and Businessman   246

Joyce C. Hall: Businessman and Greeting
Card—Maker   258

Laura Ingalls Wilder: Writer   272

Sac and Fox Indians near Saint Louis by Karl Bodmer.

State Historical Society of Missouri

Creole woman by
Anna Maria Von Phul.

Missouri Historical Society.

County Election by George Caleb Bingham.

The George Caleb Bingham home in Arrow Rock.

Watching the Cargo by George Caleb Bingham.

State Historical Society of Missouri

Order No. Eleven by George Caleb Bingham.

State Historical Society of Missouri

Canoeing on the Current River.

Missouri Division of Tourism

Aerial view of the Lake of the Ozarks.

Missouri Division of Tourism

Nichols Fountain in Kansas City.

Missouri Division of Tourism

The Gateway Arch in St. Louis.

Missouri Division of Tourism

The state seal.

Missouri Division of Tourism

The state flag.

Missouri Division of Tourism

The state flower, the hawthorn.

Missouri Division of Tourism

The state bird, the bluebird.

Missouri Division of Tourism

The state tree, the dogwood.

Missouri Division of Tourism

The state nut tree, the black walnut.

Missouri Department of Conservation

The state insect, the honeybee.

Missouri Department of Conservation

The state mineral, galena.

Missouri Division of Tourism

The state rock, mozarkite.

Missouri Division of Tourism

The state musical instrument, the fiddle.

Missouri Division of Tourism

The state fossil, the crinoid.

Missouri Department of Natural Resources; photo by Nick Decker

First Missouri State Capitol in St. Charles.

Missouri Division of Tourism

The Missouri State Capitol Building in Jefferson City.

Missouri Division of Tourism

MISSOURI
Then and Now

Chapter 1

THE FIRST MISSOURIANS

Find the answers to these questions as you read.

What Native American groups lived in Missouri? How were they alike? How were they different?

How did Indian life change after the European settlers came to Missouri?

What have the Native Americans given us?

How did Missouri get its name?

Several thousand years ago there was no United States. There was no state named Missouri. There was only a land with great forests, rolling hills, and wide rivers. It was a rich land. Early people came there to live and to hunt. Today we call those first settlers Native Americans or Indians. The American Indians were the first Missourians.

Indian people have lived in America for thousands of years. We know very little about the early Indians. They left no books to tell us how they lived. They had no way of writing as we do today.

What we know about them today comes from archaeologists. Archaeologists are scientists. They dig up the ground in places

These are some of the tools that archaeologists use. How do you think they might use each of them?

From Indians and Archaeology of Missouri *by Carl H. and Eleanor F. Chapman*

where early people once lived. They are looking for things that Missouri's first people made. Sometimes archaeologists find spear points, arrowheads, pieces of pottery, tools, and even toys. Those things are called artifacts. They also find the bones of early people and animals. By studying the artifacts and the bones they dig up, archaeologists can learn things about how Indian people lived long ago.

THE EARLY HUNTERS

What do the archaeologists know about the first people who came to Missouri? They know there were people living in America more than twenty thousand years ago. They believe those early people walked across a narrow strip of land that once connected Asia and North America. This strip is now covered by the Bering Sea and is labeled *Bering Strait* on the map on page 23. These people were hunters. They may have been searching for wild game. They probably did not know they had crossed into a new continent. During the next several thousand years these early people and their descendants traveled southward into North and South America.

The early hunters who moved into the Americas hunted large game animals. Archaeologists have found the bones of several very large animals that do not live on the earth today. Two of these early animals looked something like a very large elephant. They

Mammoth   Mastodon

The mammoth and mastodon were large prehistoric game animals.

From Indians and Archaeology of Missouri *by Chapman and Chapman*

Early hunters killed huge bison with stone-tipped spears.

were the mastodon and the mammoth. Another huge animal was the prehistoric bison. It looked like a giant buffalo.

When archaeologists dig up these old animal bones, they sometimes find Indian spear points nearby. They believe that the Native Americans used the spear points to kill the animals. Stone-tipped spears were one of the few weapons early people had for killing large game. To catch the animals, the Native Americans would frighten them. The beasts would run wildly. Sometimes the Native Americans would chase them into a marshy bog. When the big animals became stuck in the mud, the hunters killed them with their spears. For thousands of years the early hunters lived by killing the big game animals.

That changed when there were no more of the big game animals left on the earth. The spear-throwing Native Americans had to kill smaller animals for their food. They also started gathering wild plants, berries, and nuts to eat.

Often the early Indian people lived in caves. Graham Cave in Montgomery County is a Missouri cave where Native American people sometimes lived. Archaeologists have found Indian artifacts there. They found needles made of bone. The early Indians probably used them to make clothes. The archaeologists also found small handmade nets and bags. They believe the Indians used the nets to trap small game animals. They think that they may have used the bags for collecting and storing the seeds and nuts they ate. Graham Cave is an important Missouri prehistoric site. It is now a state park.

THE WOODLAND INDIANS

Many centuries passed. New groups of Indian people came to the land we call Missouri. They were different from the early hunters who only made artifacts from stone, bone, wood, and shells. The Woodland people began making clay dishes and pots. They stored food and water in their pottery.

During the Woodland period the Hopewell people came to Missouri. The Hopewells had other settlements in Ohio, Illinois, Arkansas, Louisiana, and Mississippi. We call them the Hopewells because archaeologists dug up one of their settlements on an Ohio farm owned by a family named Hopewell. There are no records to tell us the real name of the Indian people we now call the Hopewells.

The Hopewell people were mound builders. They piled up earth in the shape of large circles, half-moons, or squares. They buried their dead in these mounds. The Hopewell people probably built the mound known as "the Old Fort." It is in the Van Meter State Park in Saline County.

The Hopewell people were the first Missouri Indians to keep their settlements in the same place for a long time. They were also Missouri's first real farmers. They raised some corn. They traded some of their corn with Indian people in other parts of North America for copper and seashells. They also made clay pipes and bowls.

During the late Woodland period the Indian people began using bows and arrows instead of spears. Bows and arrows were much better for hunting smaller game animals.

5

The Mississippi people lived in well-planned cities. They usually built their cities around a large temple mound.

THE MISSISSIPPI PEOPLE (TOWN DWELLERS)

After the Hopewell people left Missouri, another group of Indian people moved into the area. They came up the Mississippi River from the south. These Native Americans lived along the rivers in the Mississippi valley. In Missouri they lived along the Mississippi and Missouri rivers. We call them the Mississippi people. We do not know what they called themselves.

The Mississippi people lived in well-planned cities and towns instead of small villages. They surrounded their cities with high fences. They built several towns along the Mississippi River near what is today St. Louis. The largest of their settlements was at Cahokia. Cahokia is in Illinois across the river from St. Louis.

The town dwellers were also mound builders. Many of their towns had a central plaza. In their plazas they built high mounds of earth that were flat on top. They put temples and other public buildings on these mounds. There were once over twenty mounds in what is now St. Louis. That is why St. Louis used to be called the

Mound City. Later settlers in St. Louis leveled off most of the mounds to make room for new buildings.

The town dwellers were excellent farmers. They had to raise enough food to feed the many people living in their towns. They made clay bottles and jars decorated with beautiful designs. They stored food and water in them. They made some pieces of pottery shaped like people and animals. The town dwellers wove cloth too. They also traded with other Native American people in North America.

When the first explorers from Europe came to Missouri, the town dwellers were gone. No one knows what happened to them. Once they left, their wood and clay buildings did not last long in the Missouri weather. Their great cities were soon gone. All that was left were the mounds.

THE NATIVE AMERICANS AND THE EUROPEANS

Explorers came to America from Europe. Europe is located across the Atlantic Ocean from North America. (The European explorers will be discussed in Chapter 3.) At first the Native Americans welcomed the explorers from the other side of the ocean. They were eager to trade with them.

The Europeans saw that some of the Indian people were wearing gold jewelry. They were looking for gold and other things that would make them rich. They wanted the valuable Native American products.

The Europeans had things that the Indian people wanted. They had guns and metal knives. These weapons were more powerful than the Indian weapons. The European explorers also brought beads, jewelry, and tools.

The Europeans brought horses, cattle, and sheep to America too. These were strange new animals that the Indians had never seen before. When the Osage Indians first saw horses, they called them "mystery dogs."

The Native Americans liked the horses. Horses made it easier for

The Europeans brought horses to America. Tribes like the Osages began using horses for hunting.

Drawing by Karl Bodmer; courtesy State Historical Society of Missouri

them to travel long distances. With horses, the Indian people did not have to carry all of their goods on their backs. The Indian women were happy because it was their job to carry most things.

The Native Americans also liked guns. The guns made it easier for them to kill animals. The Indian people traded food and furs to the Europeans for guns, axes, metal kettles, and cloth. They began using them instead of goods made from bone, stone, pottery, and animal skins.

Most North American Indian men had been hunters before the Europeans came to their land. After the traders reached America, the Native Americans began to spend even more time hunting. They needed more furs and skins to pay for trade goods. Once the Indian people killed only as many animals as they needed for food and clothing. Later they killed all the animals they could find. This meant that there were fewer wild animals. The Indian people had to travel farther to find them. Sometimes they fought with other Native Americans over hunting grounds.

Because they sold most of their animal skins to the traders, the Indian people began using blankets to keep warm. Their way of life was changing.

The European diseases were the worst problem for the Indian people. Many Native Americans died from smallpox, measles, and influenza. They had never been exposed to these diseases before. There was nothing that could be done to prevent these deaths. There were no vaccinations or medicines that could protect the Indians against the new diseases. It was a great tragedy.

THE OSAGE INDIANS

The French were the first European explorers who came to Missouri. They found two Indian tribes living there. The Osage tribe was the largest and most powerful Indian group in Missouri. There were Osage villages along the Osage River in what is today Vernon County. There were also Osage villages on the Missouri River in what is today Saline County.

The Osage people were big and strong. The men shaved their heads.

Drawing by George Catlin; courtesy State Historical Society of Missouri

Osage people were big and strong. The men shaved their heads and painted their faces. They were hunters and warriors. The Osages were already using horses when the French came to Missouri. They had gotten their horses from other Indians. Those Indians had gotten them from the Spaniards in Mexico. The Osages became excellent riders. Their children learned to ride when they were very young.

Osage hunters could shoot their bows and arrows from horseback. Each year the Osages went on three hunting trips. In early spring they hunted for bear and beaver in the Ozarks. The fur coats of these animals were thick and heavy after the long winter.

The Osages returned to their villages when it was time for the women to plant the crops. After the planting was finished, the tribe traveled to the plains west of Missouri. They spent most of the summer hunting for deer, buffalo, and elk.

In late summer the Osages went back to their villages again. The women harvested the crops they had planted in the spring. When the crops were in and stored, the Osages made their last hunting trip of the year. It lasted until the cold winter weather came.

Osage women prepared animal skins and dried the meat.

From Indians and Archaeology of Missouri *by Chapman and Chapman*

An Osage woman and her child.

State Historical Society of Missouri

Usually the entire tribe, except for the oldest members, left the villages to join the hunt. On these trips the men did the hunting. The women and children kept busy with other chores. The women prepared the animals killed by the men. They removed the skins and cleaned and tanned them. They cut up the meat and placed it on racks high above the ground to dry. The racks kept the dogs and wild animals from eating the meat. The women later made clothing from some of the skins.

Osage women did many other tasks for the tribe. The Osages considered farming to be women's work. The women had to prepare the fields and plant the crops. They planted their corn, beans, pumpkins, and squash together. At harvest time, the women cooked and dried the vegetables they had raised. Drying food kept it from spoiling. The women and children also gathered wild fruit and nuts for food.

The Osage women built the lodges. The Osage lodges were

The Osage Indians covered the outsides of their lodges with animal skins, bark, and grass mats.

From Indians and Archaeology of Missouri *by Chapman and Chapman*

about one hundred feet long. They were called long houses. The Osages covered the outside of their lodges with animal skins, bark, and grass mats. The lodges were dark and smoky inside. Ten or fifteen people lived in each of the long houses. When the Osage Indians were traveling around during their hunts, they lived in small wigwams covered with mats and animal skins. These wigwams could be easily moved from place to place. The women had to put the wigwams up and take them down every time the tribe moved during the hunt.

The Osages liked to have fun. They played games. They sang and danced. The men and boys also showed off their riding and hunting skills.

THE MISSOURI INDIANS

The Missouri Indians were another important tribe in Missouri when the French explorers arrived. Their main village was located on the Missouri River in Saline County. It was near the Missouri River Osage villages. The Missouri Indians lived much like the Osages. They hunted, farmed, and gathered wild nuts and berries.

MISSOURI'S OTHER INDIAN TRIBES

Other tribes such as the Shawnee, the Delaware, the Kickapoos, and the Peorias moved into Missouri from the east. White settlers had taken their lands. They came to Missouri looking for a new place to live. The Sac, the Fox, the Kansas, and the Ioway Indians also hunted and lived in Missouri. The color drawing on page ix shows a group of Sac and Fox Indians near St. Louis.

The Indian people got along well with Missouri's early French settlers. But later many American settlers came to Missouri. They cut down the forests to build farms. There were fewer wild animals. Finding food became difficult for the Native Americans. The Indian people did not like all of these newcomers who were moving onto their lands. Angry Native Americans and white settlers sometimes attacked each other's homes and made war.

Sadly, few of the white settlers tried to understand the Indian people's problems. The settlers only wanted to drive them away to get their land. Soon most of the Indian tribes had to leave Missouri. They moved toward the west where there were fewer settlers.

WHAT THE INDIAN PEOPLE GAVE US

Many years have passed since the Indian tribes left Missouri. But today there are still many people living in Missouri who have Indian ancestors. There are also other things to remind us that the Native Americans were Missouri's first people.

Many of the foods we eat came from them. Corn, potatoes, squash, pumpkins, beans, and tomatoes were Indian crops. Hominy, succotash, and corn bread were Indian foods. The Native Americans also gave us canoes, hammocks, and pipes. We sometimes wear Indian-style clothing like moccasins, buckskin shirts with fringe, and parkas.

We have borrowed many Indian words. Some of them are *tomahawk*, *papoose*, *hominy*, and *wigwam*. Many Missouri places also have Indian names. Kansas City, Neosho, Osceola, Miami,

FAMOUS MISSOURIANS

Big Soldier

A tall Native American warrior stood on a high hill near the Missouri River. His name was Mo'n Sho'n A-ki-Da Tonkah, which meant Great-Protector-of-the-Land. He was also called Big Soldier. Big Soldier was a leader of the Osage tribe. From the hill Big Soldier could see deer grazing nearby. There were not as many wild animals as there had once been. More settlers were moving into the area. Big Soldier was a hunter. Each year it was becoming harder to find wild game.

The settlers had brought many changes for Big Soldier and his people. These newcomers wanted the Indian people to give up their way of life. They wanted the Native Americans to become farmers and to live like the settlers. Big Soldier

and Wyaconda are cities and towns with Indian names. The Missouri, Mississippi, Osage, Niangua, and Meramec rivers also have Indian names.

OUR STATE'S NAME

Missouri itself is an Indian word. It means "the people who have big canoes." The early French settlers called the people they

knew all about the newcomers' ways. He had seen their warm homes, their gardens and fields, their cattle and horses, their wagons, and their machines. He had seen their cities. He had even traveled to the United States capital, Washington, D.C. There Big Soldier had met the great American leader, President Thomas Jefferson.

Big Soldier did not want to give up his way of life. He was proud to be a Native American. For him, the Indian way of life was the better way. The rivers and the forest gave him everything he needed. He did not wish to give up his freedom. He wanted to be able to roam through the open spaces. Big Soldier said, "I was born free, I was raised free, and I want to die free."

Most settlers never understood the Indian way of life. They thought the Indian people were lazy because they did not want to be like the settlers. The Native Americans only wanted to be themselves.

found living along the great river that flowed into the Mississippi River from the west the Missouri Indians.

The French put the word *Missouri* on their maps to mark the place where the Missouri Indians lived. Soon they also began calling the river the Missouri. Many years later the United States Congress chose the name Missouri for our state. It seems right that the state's name should have come from the Native Americans. They were the first Missourians.

New Words

archaeologist	bison	artifact
game	bog	plaza
copper	mammoth	design
prehistoric	mastodon	hominy
succotash	parka	fringe
descendant	ancestor	

 # Matching Partners

Match the right partners on a separate sheet of paper.

1. Osage Indians
2. Mississippi people
3. Early hunters
4. Hopewell people

a. the first real Indian farmers in Missouri
b. lived in large well-planned cities
c. most powerful Indian tribe living in Missouri when the first European explorers came
d. used spears to kill large game animals

✔ Testing Yourself

1. How do some scientists think the Indians came to America?

2. What kinds of animals did the earliest Indians in Missouri hunt?

3. Why did the cities of the Mississippi people disappear?

4. What were the names of some of the different tribes in Missouri after the European settlers came?

5. What were the jobs of the Osage women? What did the Osage men do?

6. What do we have today that the Indians gave us?

 Things to Talk About

1. Did the first people of Missouri know how to write like you? How have we learned about their way of life?

2. Why do we not know the names of the earliest Native American peoples?

3. Thousands of years from now, how will people be able to learn about our homes, businesses, schools, religions, and family life?

4. Have you ever found an Indian arrowhead or any Indian tools? Have you ever seen anything made by the Indians? If so, can you describe it?

5. Why do you think the Osage Indians called horses "mystery dogs" when they first saw them?

6. Look at the time line on page ii. How long is a person's lifetime? Could one person live from the time European explorers discovered America until now?

 # Things to Do

1. Pretend that you were a Native American living in Missouri when the first European explorers arrived. Write a paper telling what you think about these new people. What about them do you like? What about them do you dislike?

2. Pretend that you are an Osage Indian boy or girl. Write a paper describing your life. What do you like most about the Indian way of life?

3. Make a list of the things that the Europeans brought to Missouri that changed the Indians' way of life.

4. Draw pictures of different kinds of foods that the Indian people gave us.

 # Books You Can Read

Baird, W. David. *The Osage People*. Phoenix, Az.: Indian Tribal Series, 1972.

Coatsworth, Elizabeth. *Indian Mound Farm*. New York: Macmillan, 1969. (Fiction)

Fichter, George S. *How the Plains Indians Lived*. New York: David McKay Company, 1980.

Furman, Abraham L. *Indian Stories*. Mount Vernon, N.Y.: Lantern Press, 1974.

Glubok, Shirley. *The Art of the Plains Indians*. New York: Macmillan, 1975.

Shimer, R. H. *Scroungers: The Story of Prehistoric Americans*. Putnam's, 1971.

Whitney, Alex. *Sports and Games the Indians Gave Us*. New York: McKay, 1977.

Yellow Robe, Rosebud. *The Album of the American Indian*. New York: Franklin Watts, 1969.

A RICH LAND

Find the answers to these questions as you read.

Why did so many different Indian peoples decide to live in Missouri?

How is Missouri today different than it was when the Native Americans lived here?

What is a continent?

Where is Missouri located?

Why did fewer people settle in the Ozarks region of Missouri?

What are the two longest rivers in North America?

From earliest times Missouri has been a favorite place for settlers. It has rich soil, valuable minerals, good rivers, plenty of water, and many different plants and animals. The Native Americans were the first to discover that Missouri is a rich land. That is why so many different Indian peoples made their homes here. They came to Missouri to hunt wild animals, to gather food, to plant crops, to make salt, and to mine lead.

The land where Indian women planted corn and beans is still used for growing crops. This farmer is drill planting wheat near Mexico, Missouri.

Missouri Farm Bureau Federation

Today Missouri is different than it was when the Native Americans lived here. The rivers and the hills remain. There are still some forests. But many of the trees have been cut down to make room for farms and cities. There are factories standing in places where the Native Americans hunted wild game. Cattle graze on lands where the buffalo roamed. The lands where Indian women planted corn and beans are still used for growing crops. But Indian women dug the ground with hoes, and farmers today use tractors to plow their fields.

The Native American cities and villages are gone. They have been replaced with new towns and cities. Skyscrapers now stand where there were once Indian mounds. Some Indian trails have been turned into concrete roads and highways. The rivers that carried Indian people in canoes now transport large barges loaded with grain and other products.

LOCATING MISSOURI IN THE WORLD AND IN THE NATION

Missouri is located near the center of the North American continent. Continents are very large land masses. The earth has seven continents. The seven continents are North America, South America, Africa, Europe, Asia, Australia, and Antarctica. Find each of the continents on the map on this page.

Most of the earth's surface is covered by water. The biggest water areas are known as oceans and seas. Gulfs and lakes are also large bodies of water. Rivers are streams of water that flow through land areas into oceans, seas, gulfs, and lakes.

Now that you know what North America looks like, see if you can find North America on a globe. North America is located in the Northern Hemisphere. The equator is a great circle that divides the northern half and the southern half of the earth. The northern

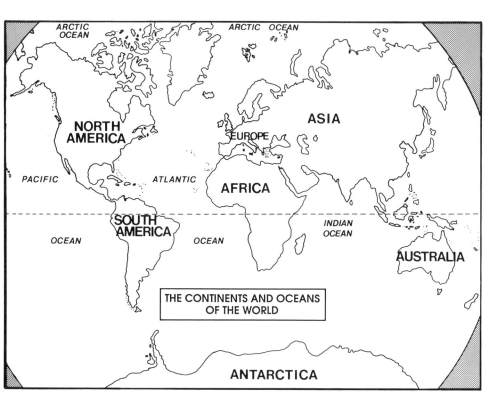

THE CONTINENTS AND OCEANS OF THE WORLD

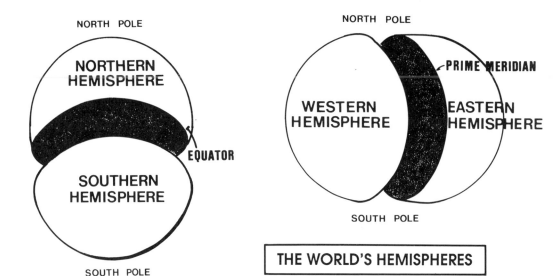

NORTH POLE

NORTHERN
HEMISPHERE

EQUATOR

SOUTHERN
HEMISPHERE

SOUTH POLE

NORTH POLE

PRIME MERIDIAN

WESTERN
HEMISPHERE

EASTERN
HEMISPHERE

SOUTH POLE

THE WORLD'S HEMISPHERES

half is called the Northern Hemisphere. The southern half is called the Southern Hemisphere. Find the equator on the globe. Now find the Northern and Southern hemispheres.

North America is also located in the Western Hemisphere. The prime meridian is a great circle passing through the north and south poles that divides the earth into the Eastern and Western hemispheres. Find the prime meridian on the globe. Now find the Eastern and Western hemispheres.

Now that you have located the North American continent, look at the bodies of water that surround it. Notice that the Atlantic Ocean lies to the east of North America, the Pacific Ocean lies to its west, the Arctic Ocean lies to its north, and the Gulf of Mexico lies to its south.

From looking at the globe, you can also see that North America is divided into several countries. The three largest countries in North America are Canada, the United States, and Mexico. Use a globe or the map on page 23 to find each of them.

You will also see that the United States is divided into fifty states. Missouri is one of the fifty states. It is located near the center of the United States. That is why Missouri is often called the "heart of America."

Missouri is bordered by eight other states. Iowa is on the north

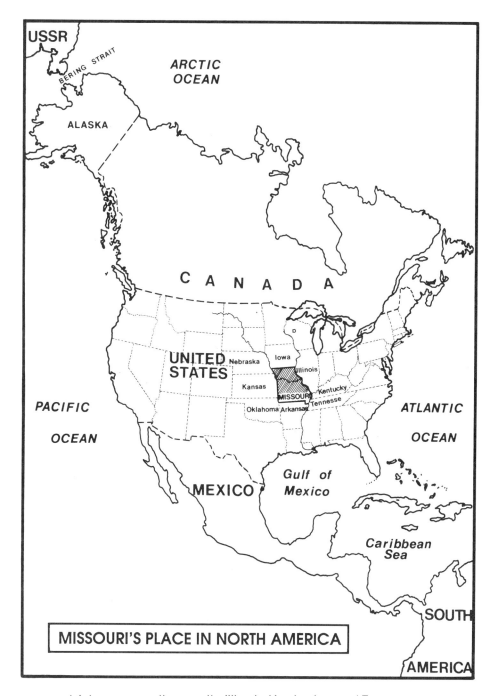

USSR

BERING STRAIT

ARCTIC
OCEAN

ALASKA

C A N A D A

UNITED
STATES

Nebraska
Iowa
Illinois
Kansas
MISSOURI
Kentucky
Oklahoma Arkansas
Tennessee

PACIFIC

OCEAN

ATLANTIC

OCEAN

MEXICO

Gulf of
Mexico

Caribbean
Sea

SOUTH

MISSOURI'S PLACE IN NORTH AMERICA

AMERICA

and Arkansas on the south. Illinois, Kentucky, and Tennessee are on
the eastern side, and Nebraska, Kansas, and Oklahoma are on
the western side.

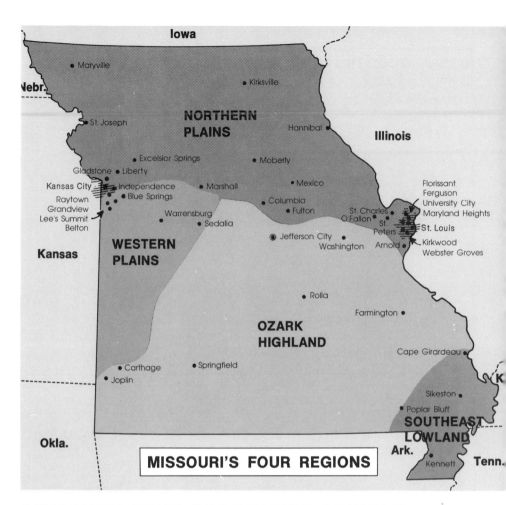

Iowa
Nebr.
Illinois
Kansas
Okla.
Ark.
Tenn.

- Maryville
- Kirksville
- St. Joseph
- Hannibal

NORTHERN
PLAINS

- Excelsior Springs
- Moberly
- Gladstone • Liberty
- Kansas City
- Independence
- Mexico
- Marshall
- Florissant
- Ferguson
- University City
- Raytown
- Blue Springs
- Columbia
- Maryland Heights
- Grandview
- Warrensburg
- Fulton
- St. Charles
- Lee's Summit
- O'Fallon
- St. Peters
- St. Louis
- Belton
- Sedalia
- Jefferson City
- Washington
- Arnold
- Kirkwood
- Webster Groves

WESTERN
PLAINS

- Rolla
- Farmington

OZARK
HIGHLAND

- Cape Girardeau
- Carthage
- Springfield
- Joplin
- Sikeston
- Poplar Bluff

SOUTHEAST
LOWLAND

- Kennett

MISSOURI'S FOUR REGIONS

MISSOURI'S FOUR GEOGRAPHIC REGIONS

The United States is made up of different regions. So is Missouri. If you have traveled to other parts of the state you have seen some of those differences. There are many kinds of land in the state. Flat lowlands lie along the rivers. In other parts of the state there are gently rolling prairies. There are also places with high, rocky hills and deep valleys. Some Missourians live in the country. Others live in small towns. Still others live in big cities.

Missouri can be divided into four regions. They are the Northern Plains, the Western Plains, the Ozark Highland, and the Southeast Lowland. Each of these regions has a different kind of land. The regions also produce different kinds of products. Find each region on the map on this page. In which region do you live?

THE NORTHERN PLAINS

Most of the Northern Plains region is located north of the Missouri River. There are many rounded hills and broad shallow valleys in the region. Long ago settlers found that the soil was good for growing crops. Many people came to the region to farm.

Today farmers in the Northern Plains grow many kinds of crops. Among them are corn, wheat, soybeans, tobacco, fruits, and vegetables. The sale of livestock is also important to farmers in this region.

The Northern Plains region has fewer mineral resources than other parts of the state. But some coal, clay, and limestone are found in the region.

Many of the largest cities in the state are located in the Northern Plains. St. Louis, St. Charles, Kansas City, Independence, Gladstone, Hannibal, Columbia, and St. Joseph are all in this region. Ballwin, Berkely, Bridgeton, Chesterfield, Clayton, Creve Coeur, Ferguson, Florissant, Hazelwood, Jennings, Kirkwood, Ladue, Maplewood, Maryland Heights, Richmond Heights, St. Ann, University City, and Webster Groves are some of the larger communities in St. Louis County. St. Peters, Mexico, Fulton, Kirksville, Liberty, Marshall, Moberly, and Maryville are also located in the Northern Plains region.

THE WESTERN PLAINS

The Western Plains region is an area of gently rolling land with only a few low hills. It is along Missouri's western border, and it is south of the Missouri River.

The farmers grow grain and raise cattle. Coal is the most important mineral in this region. Limestone, sand, and gravel are also found there.

Blue Springs, Lee's Summit, Grandview, Raytown, and Belton are all large communities close to Kansas City located near the northern edge of the Western Plains. Warrensburg and Sedalia are two other important cities in this region.

THE OZARK HIGHLAND

The Ozark Highland region is the largest one in the state. Only a few early settlers came to live in this region. The Ozark Mountains were difficult to travel through. The land was rocky and the soil was thin. It was not as good for growing crops as other regions.

Many of these early settlers came to mine lead. This region has many other mineral resources. The Ozark Highland also has large areas of zinc, iron, sand, clay, limestone, and gravel.

Forests cover much of this hilly region. Trees from the Ozark forests are used to make lumber, fence posts, fine furniture, gunstocks, and charcoal. Missouri is also the leading producer of black walnuts. The black walnut is the official state nut tree.

Some fruits and vegetables are grown in parts of the Ozarks. Farmers there raise cattle, chickens, and hogs.

The largest cities in the Ozark Highland are Springfield, Joplin,

Big Spring is the largest single spring in the United States. Each day millions of gallons of water pour from Big Spring into the Current River.

Missouri Division of Tourism

Jefferson City, Carthage, Rolla, Arnold, and Poplar Bluff. Joplin and Carthage are very near the edge of the Western Plains.

Taum Sauk Mountain, the highest point in Missouri, is in the Ozark Highland region. It is 1,772 feet high. Thousands of springs bubble up from the underground water in the Ozarks. Big Spring near Van Buren is the largest spring in the United States. Many caves are also in this lovely area. The beauty of this scenic, hilly area is very famous. Many tourists visit the Ozark Highlands every year. Look at the color photographs of the Ozarks on page xii.

THE SOUTHEAST LOWLAND

The Southeast Lowland region is sometimes called the boot-heel of Missouri. Look at the map on page 24. The shape of the lower part of the region is like the heel of a boot.

Several rivers run through the area. The land is flat, and water cannot run off easily. For many years this low, flat land was swamp-land. Many canals were built. Now the water runs into the canals and leaves the land dry enough for planting crops.

Today this land is unusually rich for growing crops. Cotton is an important crop there. Corn, wheat, soybeans, rice, and livestock are also raised in the Southeast Lowland.

The largest cities in the Southeast Lowland are Cape Girardeau, Sikeston, New Madrid, and Kennett.

MISSOURI'S RIVERS AND LAKES

Missouri is lucky to have a good supply of fresh water. Water from the faucet in your home may come from a river or lake in Missouri. Rivers are also an important way to travel. Before there were roads, rivers were the easiest way to travel. Today rivers are still used to move giant barges loaded with products.

The two longest rivers in North America come together in Missouri. They are the Mississippi and the Missouri rivers. The Missouri River begins in the Rocky Mountains. It flows almost two thousand

Missourians built canals like this in the Southeast Lowland
to drain the land. Now the land is no longer swampland.
It is some of the best farmland in the state.

Missouri Department of Conservation

The Missouri and Mis-
sissippi rivers join near
St. Louis. Look carefully
at this picture of the
two rivers. Can you see
that the Missouri River
is muddier than the
Mississippi?

Missouri Division of Tourism

MISSOURI'S RIVERS AND LAKES

miles before it cuts across the state of Missouri. It meets the Mississippi River near St. Louis. The Mississippi forms the eastern border of the state.

Missouri also has many smaller rivers. The map on this page shows the most important Missouri rivers.

Missourians use their rivers for fishing, boating, swimming, and making electricity. Huge dams have been built across some of the state's rivers. Behind each dam, a lake has been formed. Some dams can even make electric power. As the water rushes swiftly through the dam, special turbines in the dam produce electricity.

Bagnell Dam was built across the Osage River. Water collected behind the dam and formed the Lake of the Ozarks.

Missouri Division of Tourism

The largest lake in the state is Lake of the Ozarks. It was formed by building Bagnell Dam across the Osage River. Lake Pomme de Terre, Table Rock Lake, Truman Lake, and Lake Wappapello are large Missouri lakes that were also made by dams.

MISSOURI'S CLIMATE

Climate is the word used to describe the weather in a certain place over a long period of time. The temperatures and the amount of rainfall are the two most important things that determine the climate in a region. Geographers divide the world into different climate zones. Look at the world map on page 31. It shows seven different types of climate.

The polar regions are very cold, and trees will not grow there. The subarctic regions are also very cold, but they have trees and forests in them.

There are two types of temperate climate. They both have changing seasons. They also have enough rainfall for growing crops. The cool temperate climate has cold winters and warm summers. It often snows in these areas during the winter. The warm temperate climate also has winter and summer, but the winters are not as cold as in the cool temperate regions. It seldom snows in the warm temperate regions.

The dry regions have less rainfall than the temperate regions. Some parts of the dry regions have enough moisture to grow grasses and a few trees. These areas are called grasslands. The driest places are called deserts. Only a few plants will grow in the desert.

The tropical climate is both warm and wet. The highland cli-

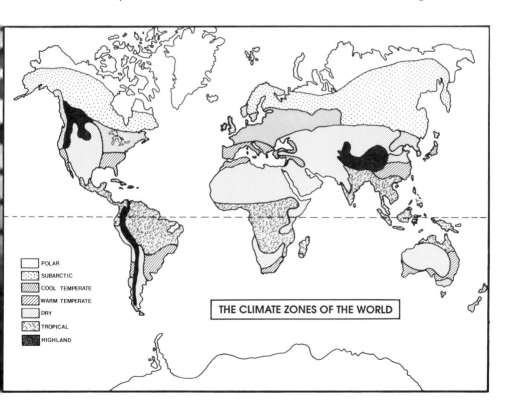

POLAR
SUBARCTIC
COOL TEMPERATE
WARM TEMPERATE
DRY
TROPICAL
HIGHLAND

THE CLIMATE ZONES OF THE WORLD

mates are found in the high mountain ranges.

Look again at the climate map on page 31. How many different climate zones are found in the United States? You can see that many parts of the United States are in the temperate zones. See if you can tell in which of these zones Missouri is located. If you chose the cool temperate zone, you were correct. Missouri has both hot summers and cold winters. But its temperatures have never stopped people from living here. Missouri's weather is warm enough to have a long growing season. In most years there is plenty of rain to water the crops and keep them healthy. That makes Missouri a good place to live.

 # New Words

buffalo	mineral resource	plains
product	spring	turbine
continent	climate	electricity
swampland	soybeans	temperate

 # Testing Yourself

1. What are the seven continents?

2. On which continent is Missouri located?

3. What country is north of the United States?

4. What country is south of the United States?

5. What states border Missouri?

6. Name Missouri's two most important rivers.

7. What is the highest point in the state?

8. What is Missouri's largest lake?

9. What type of climate does Missouri have?

Matching Partners

On a separate sheet of paper match each region with the phrase that tells something about it.

1. Northern Plains

2. Western Plains

3. Ozark Highland

4. Southeast Lowland

a. cotton is one of its most important crops

b. region north of the Missouri river

c. coal is its most important mineral resource

d. its hills are famous for their great beauty

 # Things to Talk About

1. What are some of the advantages of Missouri's central location?

2. What are the four main directions? How can you identify which direction is which? How can you tell which direction on a map is north? south? east? west?

3. Look at the map of Missouri's four regions. In which region do you live? What is the land like near your town?

4. Do you live near a large lake? Have you ever visited one of Missouri's lakes? How many different things can a lake be used for?

5. What kind of changes were caused by the construction of Bagnell Dam across the Osage River? How did those changes affect people living in that region?

6. How did the construction of drainage canals in the Southeast Lowland change life for people living in that area?

7. Which rivers in Missouri are near your community?

8. What is interesting about your town or area?

9. How do you think life would be different if you lived in a tropical climate? a desert? a polar region?

 # Things to Do

1. Draw a map of Missouri. Use different colors to show the four regions. Place a star on your map to show where your town is located. Also locate each of the following cities on your map: St. Louis, Kansas City, Springfield, Jefferson City, St. Joseph, Columbia, and Hannibal.

2. Find as many of Missouri's rivers as you can on a map of Missouri. Be sure to locate each of the following rivers: Missouri, Mississippi, Chariton, Grand, Osage, Gasconade, Meramec, St. Francis, and Current.

3. Write a paragraph about why you think Missouri is a rich land.

Books You Can Read

Banks, Marjorie, and Edith McCall. *Missouri: The Land Where Rivers Meet*. Chicago: Benefic Press, 1973.

Carpenter, Allan. *Missouri: From Its Glorious Past to the Present*. Chicago: Childrens Press, 1978.

Crisman, Ruth. *The Mississippi*. New York: Franklin Watts, 1984.

Dixon, Dougal. *Geography*. New York: Franklin Watts, 1984.

Fradin, Dennis. *Missouri: In Words and Pictures*. Chicago: Childrens Press, 1980.

Hall, Leonard. *Ozark Wildflowers*. St. Louis: Sayers Printing Co., 1969.

Lefkowitz, R. J. *Water for Today and Tomorrow*. New York: Parents Magazine Press, 1973.

McCall, Edith. *Biography of a River: The Living Mississippi*. New York: Walter and Co., 1990.

Veglahn, Nancy. *Getting to Know the Missouri River*. New York: Coward, McCann and Geoghegan, 1972.

Chapter 3

EUROPE DISCOVERS AMERICA AND MISSOURI

Find the answers to these questions as you read.

Why did the Europeans come to America?

Why did the French decide to settle in Missouri?

What were the first European settlements in Missouri?

For hundreds of years, the people of Europe had enjoyed Asian fruit and spices. Cinnamon, ginger, cloves, nutmeg, pepper, oranges, figs, and rice came from Asia. The Europeans also liked the perfumes, fine silks, beautiful carpets, and precious stones that came from the Orient.

To get these items, traders had to travel several thousand miles to the east. The trip overland was made with horses and wagons. The journey from Europe to Asia was difficult and took many months. The Europeans were anxious to find a faster and easier way to trade with the people in the Orient.

Portugal was one of the first European nations to look for a better way to get to Asia. Portuguese sailors began exploring along the African coast. They hoped to sail around Africa and on

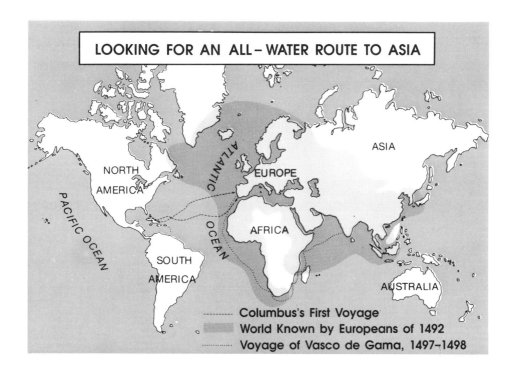

LOOKING FOR AN ALL – WATER ROUTE TO ASIA

---- Columbus's First Voyage
    World Known by Europeans of 1492
---- Voyage of Vasco de Gama, 1497–1498

to the Orient. They believed that traveling by water would be faster and easier than traveling overland. Vasco Da Gama sailed south from Portugal around Africa and on to India. He became the first European traveler to reach Asia by an all-water route. This discovery by Da Gama helped make Portugal a wealthy nation. But the voyage to India was still a long and difficult trip.

CHRISTOPHER COLUMBUS SAILS TO AMERICA

Christopher Columbus believed he knew a shorter way to get to Asia. Columbus was born in Genoa, Italy. Genoa was a port city. Ships from many places docked there. As a boy, Christopher talked with the sailors. From them he learned about ships and sailing. Christopher dreamed of sailing the oceans and seas. He studied geography to learn more about the world.

Like most educated people of his time, Columbus knew that

Christopher Columbus.

Library of Congress

the earth was round. He believed that by sailing across the Atlantic Ocean to the west he could reach Asia in just a few weeks. He hoped to establish regular trade with India and China. Many people did not think that his plan was a good one. It took him eight years to find someone who would help him. The king and queen of Spain had turned him down at first. But Queen Isabella of Spain changed her mind. She decided to give Columbus a chance to prove his point. She agreed to give him ships and money to make the trip. Queen Isabella knew that if Columbus found a shorter way to Asia, Spain would become a rich nation.

In 1492 Columbus left Spain and sailed his ships toward the west. He had three ships. They were the *Niña*, the *Pinta*, and the *Santa Maria*. Columbus sailed for over a month without seeing any land. His crews were afraid and wanted to turn back. They had given up hope of finding Asia. Suddenly, early on the morning of October 12, a sailor shouted, "Land, land." His cry awakened the others on the ship. He had seen a small island. They were all very excited. Columbus thought they had reached the East Indies off the coast of Asia. He called the people living on the island "Indians."

Columbus was wrong. He had not sailed to the East Indies. He had discovered an island off the coast of a new continent. Columbus did not know that there were two great continents between Europe and Asia. Those continents were North America and South America. Columbus died several years later still thinking that he had sailed to Asia.

SPANISH EXPLORERS IN AMERICA

The Spaniards soon knew that they had discovered a new land. A mapmaker named the new land America. He named it for Amerigo Vespucci, who was an early explorer. Spain sent many explorers to this New World in search of riches. The Spaniards found gold and silver in Mexico and in parts of South America. Spanish explorers went to many places in the Americas looking for more gold and silver. Some of them traveled far into the continent of North America, but they found no precious metals there.

As far as we know, none of these early Spanish explorers ever reached what is today Missouri. Hernando de Soto probably

Hernando de Soto discovered the Mississippi River.

Library of Congress

came the closest. He discovered the Mississippi River near where the city of Memphis stands today. When the Spanish explorers did not find what they were looking for in the center of North America, they gave up the search.

The Spaniards did not come to Missouri until many years later. But Spain did establish early settlements in other parts of the Americas. Spanish conquerors took over lands in Mexico, Central America, South America, Cuba, Santo Domingo, and several other islands in the Caribbean. The valuable metals and other products from these places made Spain a rich and powerful nation.

FRENCH EXPLORERS, TRADERS, AND MISSIONARIES

France and England watched Spain get rich from America. They also hoped to find wealth in this New World. France sent explorers to what is now Canada. These early French explorers did not find gold or silver in Canada. They did find other valuable products. The French began to trade with the Indians for furs. The furs of the beaver, otter, and mink were worth a lot of money in Europe. People there used the furs for making felt hats and for trimming fancy clothes.

The French traders traveled along the rivers into the central part of North America. There they found many Indians willing to sell them animal furs and skins.

Catholic missionaries often traveled with the French traders. The priests came to teach the Indians the Christian religion. They lived and worked among the Indians. The Indians called these priests "Black Robes."

THE DISCOVERY OF THE LAND OF MISSOURI

Louis Jolliet was a trader, and Father Jacques Marquette was a missionary. They talked to the Indian people living around the Great Lakes about the land to the west and the south. They told

Marquette and Jolliet saw many interesting sights on their journey down the Mississippi River.

Marquette and Jolliet about a great river that flowed toward the sea. They called it the Mississippi, which meant "the Father of the Waters." Marquette and Jolliet set out to find and explore the Mississippi.

They located the Mississippi with the help of their Indian guides. The French explorers paddled down the great river in two birchbark canoes. Along the way, Marquette and Jolliet saw many interesting sights. They saw giant catfish in the river. They saw wild turkeys and buffalo along the banks. They also saw an Indian painting of strange monsters on a rock ledge beside the river. Near the place where the Missouri and the Mississippi rivers came together, they visited members of the Missouri Indian tribe. Marquette and Jolliet were the first Europeans to explore in Missouri.

The Missouri Indians warned Marquette and Jolliet that the Indians farther down the Mississippi were unfriendly. The French travelers were also afraid of entering land belonging to Spain. They

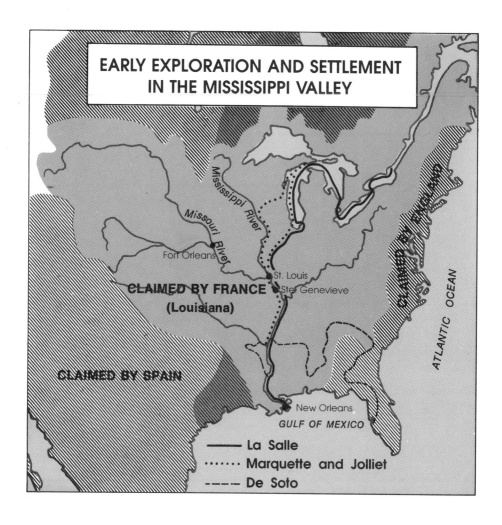

EARLY EXPLORATION AND SETTLEMENT IN THE MISSISSIPPI VALLEY

Mississippi River

Missouri River

Fort Orleans

St. Louis

Ste. Genevieve

CLAIMED BY FRANCE (Louisiana)

CLAIMED BY ENGLAND

CLAIMED BY SPAIN

ATLANTIC OCEAN

New Orleans

GULF OF MEXICO

——— La Salle

······· Marquette and Jolliet

----- De Soto

believed that the Spaniards might try to capture them. They knew that Spain did not want to share its wealth in the New World with people from other countries. So Marquette and Jolliet turned around and went back to Canada.

Soon after Marquette and Jolliet returned, another Frenchman started the same trip from Canada. His name was Robert Cavelier, sieur de la Salle. La Salle canoed all of the way down the Mississippi River to the place where it reached the Gulf of Mexico. La Salle claimed all of the land drained by the Mississippi River for the French king, Louis XIV. He named the land Louisiana in honor of King Louis. Missouri was part of Louisiana.

SETTLERS COME TO MISSOURI

More French people soon followed the early explorers to Missouri. Some of them brought black slaves with them. They traveled from Canada and other French settlements in America. Some came to trade with the Indian people for furs. A few missionaries came to teach the Native Americans about the Christian faith.

Others came looking for valuable metals. They did not find gold or silver in Missouri. They did find rich deposits of lead. The Indians had long mined for lead in Missouri. The French soon began digging for lead in the eastern Ozarks at places like Mine La Motte and Old Mines. They sold the lead, which was used for making bullets.

The French also found salt springs near Ste. Genevieve. The Indians had gone there for many years to make salt. They also hunted the animals that came there to eat the salt deposits.

French traders traveled along the rivers into the central part of North America.

State Historical Society of Missouri

The French made salt by boiling the salty water in large iron kettles. Salt was very important. People on the frontier used it for seasoning food and for preserving meat. They also used it for curing and tanning animal skins. The first French came to Missouri to operate lead mines and to make salt. They did not live in Missouri. They worked there for only part of the year. They kept homes in one of the French settlements across the Mississippi in what is now Illinois.

EARLY FRENCH SETTLEMENTS IN MISSOURI

The first French village in Missouri was located on the River Des Peres. French missionaries started this settlement. Today it would be in the southern part of the city of St. Louis. The French traders and priests lived together with the Indians at River Des Peres. When the Indians at River Des Peres decided to move back across the Mississippi River to Illinois, the settlement disappeared.

Later the French built a village on the Missouri River in the middle of Missouri. They called it Fort Orleans. Indians came to Fort Orleans to trade their furs for such things as blankets, cloth, mirrors, combs, needles, thimbles, axes, knives, iron kettles, and guns. For several years Fort Orleans was a busy trading post. The owners of Fort Orleans did not make a profit. It cost too much to run a settlement so far from the other French settlements in America. There were no other French settlements in Missouri at that time. The trade goods and supplies had to be hauled up the Mississippi and Missouri rivers all the way from New Orleans. Since they were losing money, the French decided to close Fort Orleans.

MISSOURI'S OLDEST CITY

Another early French settlement in Missouri was named Ste. Genevieve. The French left their settlements at River Des Peres and Fort Orleans after only a few years, but Ste. Genevieve is still an active community today. Ste. Genevieve is located on the Mis-

Look carefully at this painting of old Ste. Genevieve. Why do you think barrels are stacked near the water?

Painting by O. E. Berninghaus; courtesy State Historical Society of Missouri

sissippi River. It is in the southeast part of the state. It is Missouri's oldest city.

The first people settled in Ste. Genevieve about 1750. They were mostly French farmers and African slaves. They moved to Ste. Genevieve from the settlements across the river in Illinois. Missouri's rich farmland was inviting. Men, women, and children, both black and white, came to live in the new settlement. They raised corn, wheat, oats, barley, cotton, tobacco, and vegetables.

They built their houses along the riverbank. When the Mississippi flooded, their houses were filled with water. The settlers sometimes called Ste. Genevieve "Misere." *Misere* is a French word meaning misery. The great flood of 1785 was the worst one ever. The water was so deep that river travelers tied their boats to chimney tops. After that flood many residents of Ste. Genevieve decided to move their houses to higher ground farther back from the river.

The new town of Ste. Genevieve grew very rapidly. Some people built nice homes. A few of those early homes are still standing in Ste. Genevieve today. They are some of the oldest houses west of the Mississippi River. Several of them are museums that are open to the public. You can visit them and see how Missouri's early French settlers lived.

FAMOUS MISSOURIANS

Auguste Chouteau

Missouri Historical Society

Early one February morning more than two hundred years ago, fourteen-year-old Auguste Chouteau watched as workers began chopping down trees. They had begun clearing the land for a new settlement. The settlement was St. Louis. Pierre Laclede had chosen young Chouteau to be charge of the project. Laclede was sure that this French boy could carry out the important task.

Chouteau did not disappoint him. He carefully followed Laclede's directions. The workers built several log cabins. They also built a stone trading post with some help from the Missouri Indians who had come to watch them. In a short time the new settlement began to take shape in the wilderness.

For the next sixty-five years, Auguste Chouteau watched and helped St. Louis grow into a great city. Chouteau became an important fur trader. For many years he traded with the Osage Indians. They made him an honorary member of their tribe. His St. Louis warehouses were filled with valuable furs. He conducted business with merchants in England, Canada, and the United States. Chouteau became Missouri's largest landowner. He also helped start the first bank in Missouri.

Chouteau was more than a successful trader and businessman. He served as an Indian agent for Spain and later for the United States. The United States bought the Louisiana Territory in 1803. Chouteau worked with the new American government. Missouri's new leaders often came to him for help. He helped the United States make treaties with the Indians. He served as a judge. He was also a member of the territorial Legislative Council, the St. Louis Board of Trustees, and the St. Louis School Board.

Chouteau and his family lived in a big two-story stone house near the Mississippi River in downtown St. Louis. It was the finest home in early St. Louis. The Chouteaus owned nice pieces of furniture, fancy mirrors, fine paintings, and a beautiful crystal chandelier. Some of those things had been brought to St. Louis from France. Chouteau and his wife, Therese, often had important guests in their home. On special occasions they set their table with fancy tablecloths, fine china, and sterling silver.

Unlike many people on the frontier, Chouteau was a well-educated man. He had a very large library in his home. He read books on many different subjects.

Chouteau's family was large. He and Therese had nine children. Auguste Chouteau was a successful family man, trader, and community leader.

THE FOUNDING OF ST. LOUIS

Pierre Laclede was a French merchant in New Orleans. He wanted to trade with the Indians living along the Missouri and Mississippi rivers. He and his business partner decided to set up a trading post and settlement near the mouth of the Missouri. Laclede chose a place on the Mississippi River for the new settlement.

In 1764 he sent his clerk, Auguste Chouteau, there to clear the land and build the first buildings. Laclede sent thirty men with Chouteau to do the work. Chouteau was only fourteen years old, but Laclede put him in charge of the workers. Laclede named the new town St. Louis. In a short time, St. Louis became an important fur trading center.

St. Louis is the second oldest city in Missouri, and it is one of America's great cities.

 New Words

perfumes	furs	missionary
kettle	island	canoe

✔ Testing Yourself

1. What were both Christopher Columbus and Vasco Da Gama looking for?

2. What were the names of Columbus's ships?

3. Why did Columbus call the people he found in the Americas *Indians*?

4. What did the early Spanish explorers hope to find in North America?

5. Why did the early French explorers and settlers come to Missouri?

6. Why was salt an important product in early Missouri?

7. Who were the first settlers in Ste. Genevieve?

8. Why was St. Louis founded?

 ## Fill in the Blanks

Write the following sentences on another sheet of paper. Fill each blank with the correct word.

1. ▬▬▬▬ ▬▬▬▬ discovered America.

2. A fur trader named ▬▬▬▬ ▬▬▬▬ and a missionary named ▬▬▬▬ ▬▬▬▬ led the first French expedition to Missouri.

3. The oldest city in Missouri is ▬▬▬▬ ▬▬▬▬.

4. The fourteen-year-old boy who helped Pierre Laclede start St. Louis was ▬▬▬▬ ▬▬▬▬.

5. St. Louis soon became the center of the ▬▬▬▬ ▬▬▬▬.

 ## Things to Talk About

1. If you had been a Native American living in Missouri, what would you have thought about Father Jacques Marquette and Louis Jolliet?

2. If you had been with Louis Jolliet and Jacques Marquette, what things about their famous trip would you have found most exciting?

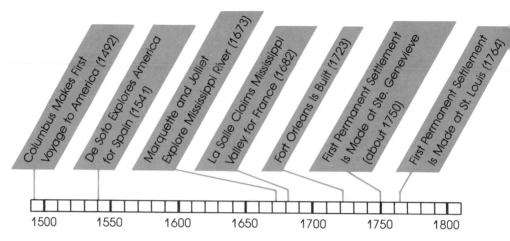

1500	1550	1600	1650	1700	1750	1800

 ## Using a Time Line

1. On another sheet of paper, put these events in the order they happened. Be sure to look at the time line on this page.

   De Soto's journey through America

   Columbus's first voyage

   Founding of St. Louis

   Marquette and Jolliet's trip down the Mississippi

   Founding of Ste. Genevieve

   La Salle's trip to the mouth of the Mississippi

2. Using what you have learned in this chapter, decide if these people could have ever met Louis Jolliet: Christopher Columbus, La Salle, and Auguste Chouteau. Explain the reasons for your answer. Keep in mind the number of years a person can be expected to live.

Books You Can Read

Abodaher, David J. *French Explorers of North America*. New York: Julian Messner, 1970.

Baker, Nina Brown. *A Boy for a Man's Job: The Story of the Founding of St. Louis*. Philadelphia: Winston, 1952.

Buchheimer, Naomi. *Let's Go Down the Mississippi with LaSalle*. New York: Putnam's, 1962.

Buehr, Walter. *French Explorers in America*. New York: Putnam's, 1961.

———. *The Spanish Conquistadors in North America*. New York: Putnam's, 1962.

Cooper, Kay. *Journeys on the Mississippi*. New York: Julian Messner, 1981.

Greene, Carol. *Christopher Columbus: A Great Explorer*. Chicago: Childrens Press, 1989.

Heimann, Sue. *Christopher Columbus*. Chicago: Childrens Press, 1974.

McCall, Edith. *Explorers in a New World*. Chicago: Childrens Press, 1980.

Stein, R. Conrad. *The Story of Marquette and Jolliet*. Chicago: Childrens Press, 1981.

Syme, Ronald. *De Soto: Finder of the Mississippi*. New York: William Morrow, 1957.

———. *Marquette and Jolliet: Voyagers on the Mississippi*. New York: William Morrow, 1974.

Chapter 4

LIFE IN FRENCH MISSOURI

Find the answers to these questions as you read.

What was life like in Missouri's early French villages?

Why were African-Americans so important in French Missouri?

How did the settlers in French Missouri get along with their Indian neighbors?

How did the people in French Missouri make their livings?

What special jobs did women have in French Missouri?

What did people do for fun in French Missouri?

Today people from many different places live in Missouri. As you have learned, the Indians were the state's first people. French and African settlers were the next to arrive. French fur traders, missionaries, lead miners, and farmers followed the first French explorers to Missouri. Some black slaves came with them. Most of the slaves also spoke French.

Many people from England came to America and settled along the Atlantic Ocean. Over the years the English-speaking people moved westward from the coast into the heart of America. But the English arrived in Missouri many years after the first French and African settlers.

THE FRENCH VILLAGE

Red, white, and black settlers lived together in villages along the Mississippi and Missouri rivers. The French villages in Missouri were quite different from American towns. The Americans put their stores and shops in a business district. They built their homes in another part of town. The French mixed their homes, stores, and public buildings throughout the village. French merchants used their homes as their places of business.

The French did not build their houses close together. They surrounded their houses with slave cabins, barns, stables, orchards, and gardens. The French built a fence made of cedar posts around each house and its grounds. The fences kept out wild animals and stray livestock.

FRENCH HOUSES

A few wealthy French people built stone houses. But most French houses were made of logs. A log house was the easiest kind of house to build. The French log house was different from the American log cabin. The French placed their logs upright like fence posts. American log cabins were built with the logs laid lengthwise. The French filled the cracks between the logs with mud, twigs, and animal hair. They often painted the walls with whitewash.

Most French houses were only one story high. They had very steep roofs. The very first French buildings in America used grass mats to cover the roofs. Because the roofs were so steep, the

The Bequette-Ribault house in Ste. Genevieve is one of the oldest French-style houses in the United States. Many early French houses in Missouri looked like it does today.

Photograph by Jack E. Boucher for the Historic American Buildings Survey, Washington, D.C.

rainwater ran off very quickly. The water ran too fast to drip through the roof and get the inside of the house wet. The grass roofs could catch on fire very easily. Bugs and mice also built nests in the grass mats. Sometimes the bugs and mice fell out of the roofs into the room. Before long French builders began replacing the grass mats with wooden shingles. But they kept the steep rooflines on their houses.

The French also built porches around their houses. The French called these porches "galleries." The porches kept the plaster walls dry when it rained. They also helped shade the house from the hot summer sun. Many French houses also had wooden shutters. They could be closed over the windows in bad weather. Fireplaces were used for heating and for cooking.

Most of the houses were small and plain. Some were one-room buildings with dirt floors. Others were two-room houses, with wooden floors and a loft above. Most of them contained only a few pieces of furniture. Inside most French houses, you would find

The Bolduc house in Ste. Genevieve has been carefully restored. Notice the fence of cedar posts around the house.

Missouri Division of Tourism

This is a picture of the inside of the Bolduc house today. The
French used only a few simple pieces of furniture.

Photograph by Jack E. Boucher for the Historic American Buildings Survey, Washington, D.C.

FAMOUS MISSOURIANS

Jeanette Fourchet

Early St. Louis was a frontier village where red, white, and black people lived together. Most of the African-Americans in early St. Louis were slaves. But there were also some free black people who lived and worked there. Jeanette Fourchet was a free black woman in St. Louis. She owned a house on Second Street and a piece of farmland in the common field. She had cows and other farm animals. She also owned clothes, furniture, dishes, large iron kettles, irons, and other household goods.

Since she owned irons and large kettles, she probably earned a living by doing laundry for people in St. Louis. She may also have helped take care of sick people. She owned a mortar and pestle, which could have been used for making medicine.

Fourchet was a Catholic. She had four children. Her first husband, Gregory, died. She married Valentine, who was a free black man. He was a gunsmith and a trapper. He had a license from the Spanish government giving him permission to trap and hunt. As a hunter Valentine sometimes roamed in the woods in search of game. He became ill and died at an Osage Indian village during one of those hunting trips.

Jeanette Fourchet died in St. Louis the year that the United States bought the Louisiana Territory. She left her property to her children and grandchildren. Fourchet's story is important because it tells us something about the life of free black people in Missouri.

a few chairs, a table, beds, a chest for storing clothes, and a cupboard for storing dishes.

A few wealthy French people lived in bigger and finer homes. Auguste Chouteau's large home in St. Louis had polished walnut floors and a glass chandelier from France.

Have you ever seen an early French-style house? You can usually spot an old French house by looking at its porches and its roof. The Bolduc and the Bequette-Ribault houses in Ste. Genevieve are good examples. They are museums today. People travel from all over the United States to visit them.

AFRICAN-AMERICANS IN MISSOURI'S EARLY FRENCH COMMUNITIES

From early times African-Americans lived and worked in Missouri. About one of every three people living in the French settlements at Ste. Genevieve and St. Louis was an African-American. Most of them were slaves. They helped build Missouri. Black slaves mined lead, cleared land, planted and cultivated crops, made salt, hunted and trapped, and rowed boats. Some held jobs as carpenters and skilled workers. Others worked as cooks, housekeepers, and servants. As slaves, they had to work for their masters. Their life was hard, and they had very little freedom. (In Chapter 10 you will read more about slavery.)

Not all African-Americans in early Missouri were slaves. There were a few free blacks. Some had been set free by their masters as a reward for their years of hard work. Others had managed to earn enough money to buy their own freedom by hiring themselves out during their few spare hours. The free black men worked as hunters, rowers, traders, and craftsmen. The free black women worked as housekeepers and servants. Free blacks owned property and used the courts to collect money that people owed them.

Auguste Chouteau's large home in St. Louis had polished walnut floors and a glass chandelier. It was torn down in 1841.

Lithograph by J. C. Wild; courtesy Missouri Historical Society

THE FRENCH AND THEIR INDIAN NEIGHBORS

The French got along well with the Native Americans. They traded with them. They sold them guns and other French goods. Because there were few French settlers in America, they did not try to take the land from the Indians. Sometimes there were problems between the French settlers and the Indian people. But most of the time the two groups lived together in peace.

The Indian people opened their lodges to the French hunters and traders who came to their villages to sell trade goods for furs. Many traders had Indian wives. Louis Lorimier was a famous trader. His father was a Frenchman, and his mother was a Native American. Lorimier started the town of Cape Girardeau. He was married to a Shawnee Indian woman. Their son later went to the U.S. Military Academy at West Point.

Indian people often came to Missouri's French villages to do business or to meet with government officials. A few Native Americans even lived in the French settlements. A small group of Peoria Indians lived in cabins in the village of Ste. Genevieve.

The Shawnee Indians settled near the French villages in Missouri. Where do you think this Shawnee man got the blanket he is wearing?

Native American women frequently came to the French settlements to sell moccasins and other Indian goods.

*Drawing by Anna Maria von Phul;
courtesy Missouri Historical Society*

The French used two-wheeled carts for hauling crops and other things.

Drawing by Anna Maria von Phul; courtesy Missouri Historical Society

Several Indian tribes had moved to Missouri from the east. Many of them settled near the French settlements. Stephen Austin grew up in Potosi. He remembered playing games with the Indian children. They came with their parents to the store owned by Stephen's father. Henry Brackenridge was a young American boy who came to Ste. Genevieve to learn French. While he was there, his Indian playmates taught him how to shoot a bow and arrow.

The Indians and their neighbors in Missouri borrowed from each other. The Indian people liked the metal tools, guns, blankets, clothing, and jewelry that they got from the French traders. The French settlers often wore moccasins and leather pants that the Native Americans made and sold. Both white and black settlers grew and ate Indian foods such as corn, beans, pumpkins, and squash. Indian hunters sold them wild game they had killed. Some French people could speak and understand Indian languages. Some Indian people could speak and understand French. They also borrowed words and sayings from each other.

FARMING IN FRENCH AMERICA

Most of Missouri's early French settlers were farmers. American farmers owned their own farms. French farmers planted their crops in a field owned by the whole village. It was called the common field. The common field was usually just outside the village. Each family received a strip of land in it. Everyone had to help keep up the fence around the common field.

The French farmers and their slaves grew many different crops. They raised wheat, corn, cotton, flax, hemp, and tobacco in the common field. They also grew fruits and vegetables in the orchards and gardens near their homes.

All the village farm animals grazed in the same pasture. The French cut their firewood in a common forest.

FUR TRADING AND LEAD MINING

As you already know, fur trading was very important in early Missouri. French fur traders traveled up the Mississippi and Missouri rivers in small boats and canoes. The traders would swap supplies with the Indians for furs. St. Louis became an important place for

Lead mining was hard work. French and African-American workers operated lead mines in early Missouri.

Walker, Missouri Resources Division; courtesy State Historical Society of Missouri

selling furs. The merchants there bought and sold furs. Auguste Chouteau and his brother Pierre became wealthy men by trading furs.

Lead mining was also important in early Missouri. Philippe Renault ran the lead mines near Ste. Genevieve. This was before there were any villages in Missouri. Renault had slaves who did much of the work. Lead from Missouri mines is still important today.

WOMEN IN FRENCH MISSOURI

Women had to take care of their families. They had to prepare the food. They made and took care of the clothing and kept their houses clean. Preparing food included planting and caring for gardens, harvesting and preserving vegetables and fruit, milking cows, baking bread, and cooking meals.

Women also had to take care of the children. Families were large. Most families had several children. There were very few doctors in the French settlements. Women had to look after people who were sick or hurt. These many tasks kept women busy most of the time. It was very hard on slave women. They had to do the chores for their families after they had worked all day for their owners.

French women in Missouri had more to say about business than most English women in the American colonies. The French men often worked away from their homes trading, hunting, and mining. Wives had to take care of business matters while their husbands were gone. The French laws also gave women more rights to take care of their property than the English laws.

FRENCH COOKING

The women in French Missouri were good cooks. They learned to use the new foods in America to make delicious meals. The French liked gumbos, stews, and soups more than roasted and fried meats. Gumbos came from Africa. This is an example of how the African-Americans influenced the French diets. The Indian women also introduced Indian foods into the local diet. Hominy, succotash, and corn bread were all Indian dishes. But the French liked wheat bread better than corn bread.

The cooks in Missouri had many different foods to choose from. There usually was plenty of food for all. The people raised potatoes, pumpkins, turnips, corn, melons, cabbages, beets, peas, and carrots. They grew apples, peaches, plums, and grapes in their orchards. They also gathered nuts and berries in the forests. Food was sweetened with wild honey or sugar made from maple-tree sap. Lard and bear grease were used for cooking.

The settlers raised cattle, hogs, and chickens. From these they could get meat, milk, eggs, and butter. Good hunters could also find wild game in the nearby woods. Bear, deer, raccoon, squirrel, opossum, duck, turkey, quail, and pheasant were often served. The streams and rivers provided a rich supply of fish.

FRENCH CLOTHING

The French in Missouri usually dressed in very simple clothes. The women made the clothes that their families wore. French women were different from other pioneer women in one interesting way. They did not spin their own thread and weave their own cloth. They had it brought to America from France. There were almost no spinning wheels or looms in the French houses in Missouri.

For everyday dress the French men wore pants made from buckskin or rough cotton. They also wore loose-fitting cotton shirts, blue handkerchiefs on their heads, and leather moccasins. During cold weather the men put on a heavy cape with a hood. It was called a *capot*. They also wore fur hats and fur mittens.

The everyday clothes women wore were also simple. They usually wore long red or blue cotton skirts and a short cotton jacket. They also wore a long cotton cape called a *pelisse* with a white or blue handkerchief on the head, and moccasins. In the winter the women wore heavy wool jackets. The painting on page ix shows a French woman wearing everyday clothes.

On Sundays and holidays the French villagers wore their fancy clothes. The richer people wore clothes made from silk, satin, and velvet. Some women had special dresses trimmed with ribbons and lace. On special days the women also wore earrings, ivory combs in their hair, silk stockings, and fancy slippers. The wealthy men dressed up in fancy coats with gold buttons and leather dress shoes with buckles. A few rich families had clothes made in France.

FRENCH SCHOOLS

Most children in French Missouri did not go to school. Free schools for all children had not yet been started. There were only a few schools. Students had to pay to attend them. These schools were mostly for beginners. Only the richest families could afford to give their children more schooling. Some important French people sent their children to schools in Canada or the United States.

The French settlers enjoyed music and dancing.

State Historical Society of Missouri

FRENCH PEOPLE AT PLAY

The French were fun-loving people. Horse racing was a favorite sport. The French liked music and dancing. Their favorite dances were reels, minuets, waltzes, and two-steps. They also enjoyed playing games and telling stories. Everyone in the village usually went to the dances and parties. They were held in most French villages on Sundays and special holidays.

The people were almost all Catholics. The Catholic church played an important part in Missouri's early history. On religious holidays there were special family and village festivals.

New Year's Eve was a special day in the French communities. On that night the people danced from house to house. As they danced, they sang an old French song called *La Guignolee*. The French villagers had to work hard. But they still found time to enjoy themselves.

THE VALLE FAMILY OF STE. GENEVIEVE

The people of Ste. Genevieve frequently met at the home of Francois Valle II. He was the most important official in Ste. Genevieve. His father had also been a leader in the town. The people of Ste. Genevieve liked and trusted the Valles.

Francois Valle II and his wife, Marie Carpentier Valle, had four-teen children. Seven of their children died before they were five years old.

Marie Carpentier Valle knew more about childhood illnesses than almost anyone in Ste. Genevieve. Mothers in the community came to her for advice when their children were sick. Often there was no doctor in Ste. Genevieve.

The Valles were wealthy. Valle was a merchant. He sold goods in Ste. Genevieve from New Orleans and from Europe. He also made money from lead mining, salt making, farming, and grist and saw milling. The Valles owned much land. They also owned many slaves. The Valles let their slaves carry guns. That was very unusual. The Valles believed that their slaves needed guns for protection on the frontier.

Francois Valle II died only a few days before Ste. Genevieve became a part of the United States. Valle knew that French Missouri was changing. Many Americans had already begun to settle there. Francois had sent one of his sons to school in New York so that he could learn English. Valle understood that Missouri would soon be a different place.

New Words

merchant	shutters	plaster
cupboard	moccasin	whitewash
gumbo	chandelier	shingles
carpenter	loft	license
mortar and pestle	lard	

Choose the Right Words

Select the right words to make each of these sentences correct. Then write the sentences correctly on another sheet of paper.

1. The first European settlers in Missouri were (French, English, Spanish).

2. The early French settlers in Missouri lived (in villages, on farms that were far apart).

3. Most early French settlers lived in houses they built from (brick, stone, logs).

4. The French settlers often wore (moccasins and leather pants, metal jewelry) that the Indians made and sold.

5. The early French settlers ate mostly (stews and soups, fried meats, food from France).

6. (Gumbo, hominy) was a food that came from Africa.

7. French lead mining was most important around (St. Louis, Ste. Genevieve).

 # True or False

Some of these sentences are true, and some are false. On another sheet of paper, rewrite the false statements and make them true.

1. Most French houses were one story high.

2. Early French houses in Missouri were exactly like those built by American settlers.

3. Most French families had only one child.

4. The French settlers sometimes wore fancy clothes for Sundays and holidays.

5. Most French children did not have a chance to go to school.

6. Most French settlers in Missouri were Catholics.

7. All African-Americans in early Missouri were slaves.

8. The French did not take time out for fun.

Things to Talk About

1. Have you ever been to Ste. Genevieve? If you have, tell about some of the things you saw there.

2. What were some of the most important differences between the French and American settlers in early Missouri?

 # Things to Do

1. Make a list of all the places in Missouri you can think of that have French names.

2. Make believe that you are living in an early French village in Missouri. Write a paragraph about how you might spend a day.

 # Books You Can Read

Baker, Nina Brown. *A Boy for a Man's Job: The Story of the Founding of St. Louis*. Philadelphia: Winston, 1952.

Wooldridge, Rhoda. *Chouteau and the Founding of Saint Louis*. Independence, Mo.: Independence Press, 1975. (Fiction)

———. *And Oh! How Proudly*. Independence, Mo.: Independence Press, 1972. (Fiction)

Chapter 5

MISSOURI BECOMES A PART OF THE UNITED STATES

Find the answers to these questions as you read.

What European nations owned the land called Missouri?

How did Missouri become a part of the United States?

What kind of disagreement kept Missouri from becoming a state earlier?

Why did Missourians write a constitution in 1820?

Spain and France claimed land in the New World. England did also. The English established most of their settlements in North America along the coastline of the Atlantic Ocean.

During the 1700s, France, Spain, and England each wanted to be the strongest power in the world. They fought several wars. These wars usually began in Europe, but some battles were fought in America. They were fighting for the right to control the lands in America. After one great war ended, France had to give Canada to England. France also gave Louisiana to Spain. Missouri was a part of the land called Louisiana. Missouri was no longer a French colony. Spain now ruled Missouri.

THE AMERICAN REVOLUTION

European leaders found that it was difficult to rule colonies from across the ocean. The English colonists in North America were unhappy with the way England ruled them. They did not like many of the laws the English government made for them. They said that they were not represented in England's lawmaking body. The English-Americans believed that they were losing the rights that belonged to all English people. In 1776, Thomas Jefferson wrote a paper called the Declaration of Independence. The Americans used it to announce that they no longer wanted to be a part of England. They said that they intended to establish a new country with a government controlled by the people.

England did not want to lose its North American colonies. The English sent an army to America to force the colonists to accept English rule. The Americans fought to win their freedom. This war was called the American Revolutionary War.

The American Revolutionary War soldiers fought bravely against the English army.

Library of Congress

The leader of the American army was General George Washington. It was a difficult fight for the Americans. The French helped them by sending ships, soldiers, and supplies. French leaders saw this as a way to get even with England for taking Canada away from them.

After several years of fighting, the English decided to make peace with their American colonies. They agreed to let the Americans form their own country. The Americans called their new country the United States of America. The people elected George Washington to be their first president. In the peace treaty, England allowed the United States to have the land between the Atlantic Ocean and the Mississippi River.

AMERICAN SETTLERS IN MISSOURI

Missouri was on the other side of the Mississippi River. It still belonged to Spain. Few Spaniards had come to live in Missouri. The Spanish officials wanted more settlers. They invited Americans to live in Missouri. They promised them free land and no taxes.

Daniel Boone was a famous American who accepted the Spanish offer. He moved to Missouri from Kentucky. Boone was already a well-known pioneer and trailblazer. As a young boy Daniel liked to be in the woods. He learned how to handle a rifle. He also learned how to move quietly through the forest. He learned the ways of the Indians. As he grew older Boone tried to settle on a farm. But he did not like farming. He liked to hunt better.

Daniel Boone fell in love with Rebecca Bryan. They got married. The Boones went to Kentucky. They were some of the first American settlers there. They had many problems with the Indians. Daniel was often gone. Rebecca Boone had to take care of their family. She was also a good pioneer. She knew how to mold bullets, shoot a gun, and skin a deer.

The Boones had ten children. One of their children died as a baby. Two other Boone children were killed by Indians. Their son Daniel Morgan Boone was the first member of the family to come

Daniel Boone was a famous American pioneer and trailblazer. He spent his last years in Missouri.

Missouri Historical Society

to Missouri. He urged his parents to settle in Missouri. He said it was beautiful country.

Daniel Boone liked the idea of moving to Missouri. He was getting old, but he still did not like to stay in one place. Daniel and Rebecca joined their son in Missouri. Several of their children, grandchildren, and friends followed them to Missouri. The Spaniards gave Boone a large piece of land and also appointed him to be a judge. They believed that other American settlers would follow the famous Boone family to Missouri. Many of them did. Missouri soon had more American settlers than French and Spanish settlers.

Daniel and Rebecca Boone spent the rest of their lives in Missouri. Daniel hunted and made salt in the woods with his sons. Daniel Boone was an old man when he died at the home of his

Nathan Boone built this house near Defiance. His father, Daniel Boone, died there in 1820.

Missouri Division of Tourism

son Nathan. Today Nathan Boone's home is a historic site. It is located near Defiance in St. Charles County.

THE LOUISIANA PURCHASE

In 1799 Napoleon Bonaparte became the ruler of France. Napoleon wanted to build a new French empire. He hoped to get back some of the colonies France had lost in North America. He made a deal with Spain. Spain agreed to return the Louisiana Territory to France in exchange for some land in Europe that France controlled. Two years later officials in New Orleans said that the Americans could no longer unload their boats there.

Many western Americans were worried. For years they had

floated their products down the Mississippi River on flatboats. When they reached New Orleans they sold their goods. The westerners wanted the American government to help them keep New Orleans open for their boats.

Thomas Jefferson was president of the United States. He sent two American officials to France to talk with the French leaders about the problem. The Americans told the French that the United States wanted to buy New Orleans. Instead, the French ruler, Napoleon, offered to sell the United States all of the Louisiana Territory. Napoleon had lost interest in America. He also needed money. The Americans were very surprised and very pleased. They agreed to buy the Louisiana Territory.

In 1803 the United States paid France fifteen million dollars for the Louisiana Territory. Louisiana covered a large area. The pur-

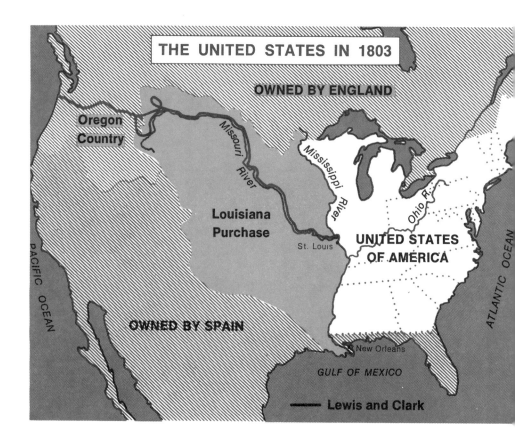

THE UNITED STATES IN 1803

OWNED BY ENGLAND

Oregon Country

Missouri River

Mississippi River

Ohio R.

Louisiana Purchase

St. Louis

UNITED STATES OF AMERICA

PACIFIC OCEAN

ATLANTIC OCEAN

OWNED BY SPAIN

New Orleans

GULF OF MEXICO

—— Lewis and Clark

Thomas Jefferson was president of the United States at the time of the Louisiana Purchase. Missouri's capital city is named for him.

Painting by George Caleb Bingham; courtesy State Historical Society of Missouri

chase doubled the size of the United States. The Americans got a real bargain. This valuable land cost the United States only a few cents an acre.

Missouri was part of Louisiana. The Louisiana Purchase was a very important event for Missourians. It made them citizens of the United States.

RAISING THE AMERICAN FLAG

Officials in St. Louis held a special ceremony to transfer the Louisiana Purchase to the United States. Many people gathered to watch the raising of the American flag. Some of the old French residents had tears in their eyes. They knew that American rule would bring changes.

Captain Amos Stoddard represented the United States at the ceremony. He promised Missourians that they would now enjoy all the rights of American citizens.

FAMOUS MISSOURIANS

Meriwether Lewis

Missouri Historical Society

William Clark

State Historical Society of Missouri

Meriwether Lewis and William Clark

It was a warm spring morning in 1804. The crews pushed the three boats away from the riverbank at St. Charles. The forty-some men in the boats were heading up the Missouri River on their way to the Pacific Ocean.

For weeks Meriwether Lewis and William Clark had been getting ready for the trip. They had packed food, clothing, medicines, guns, gunpowder, knives, axes, and lead for bullets. They also carried presents to give the Indians they expected to meet. They even had a thermometer. A St. Louis doctor had made it for them by scraping the mercury for it from the back of his wife's mirror.

Only a few months before, the United States had bought Louisiana from France. The size of the young nation had suddenly doubled. American leaders did not know much about this land. Very few people besides Indians had traveled deep into Louisiana.

President Thomas Jefferson chose Lewis and Clark to explore the land. Jefferson wanted them to follow the Missouri River as far as they could. Then he wanted them to go to the Pacific Ocean. They were to write down everything they saw and did.

Jefferson made wise choices. Meriwether Lewis had been his secretary. The president knew that Lewis would do a good job. Lewis had suggested his friend William Clark to be the other leader. The two men were good friends. They worked well together.

The group of explorers faced many dangers. They fought off grizzly bears and rattlesnakes. They crossed steep, snow-covered mountains. Their boats turned over in fast-running rivers. Storms and bad weather slowed them down. Food sometimes was hard to find. They had to eat bear grease, boiled roots, and dog meat.

Along the way they met thousands of Indian people. Most of them were friendly. Sacajawea was an Indian woman who traveled with them. Her husband was a French trader who also went along. Sacajawea had once lived in the land Lewis and Clark were planning to explore. She acted as an interpreter. She spoke the languages of some of the tribes Lewis and Clark visited. Clark's African-American slave York also made the trip.

Lewis and Clark finally reached the Pacific Ocean eighteen months after they started. The trip back to Missouri did not take them as long. It was faster and easier to travel down the Missouri River. They did not have to row against the strong river currents.

The trip to the Pacific and back took twenty-eight months. The explorers had been gone so long that the people in St. Louis thought they had all died. Everyone was happy to see that they were alive and well when they returned to St. Louis.

Lewis and Clark had many stories to tell. They told about Sacajawea and the Native Americans they had met. They described the many different kinds of plants and animals they had seen. They also talked about how big and beautiful the West was. They gave the United States much information about the new land.

Later, both Lewis and Clark became important Missouri leaders. President Jefferson named Lewis to be governor of the Missouri Territory. He appointed Clark to lead Missouri's militia. Clark was also an Indian agent. Most Indians liked and respected Clark. They called him the "Red Head." Several years after Lewis's death, Clark also became governor of the Missouri Territory. He lived in St. Louis for the rest of his life. He sometimes showed visitors the Indian souvenirs, animal skins, elephant tusks, and other unusual things he had collected.

Many people gathered to watch the raising of the American flag in St. Louis after the Louisiana Purchase.

State Historical Society of Missouri

Sacajawea was an Indian woman who traveled with Lewis and Clark. She helped them interpret Indian languages.

State Historical Society of Missouri

Meriwether Lewis and William Clark watched the transfer ceremony. They were in St. Louis getting ready for a long trip across the North American continent. They planned to explore the Missouri River to the northwest. They also hoped to reach the Pacific Ocean. President Jefferson had asked them to make this trip.

MORE AMERICANS COME TO MISSOURI

More Americans began coming to Missouri. They were eager to make Missouri their home now that it was part of the United States. Thousands of new settlers traveled to Missouri on boats and in wagons. St. Louis, St. Charles, and the other river towns were often crowded with newcomers.

These new settlers brought many changes to Missouri. Missouri's French villages began to look more like American towns. The Americans built new two-story American brick buildings next to the old French houses.

New settlers traveled as far as they could by water.

A wagon pulled by a team of oxen often took the settlers from the river to their new homes.

State Historical Society of Missouri

Fort Osage in Jackson County was an early fort and trading post operated by the United States.

State Historical Society of Missouri

The Americans also opened new businesses. The French merchants had sold goods from their homes. The Americans had stores with signs attached to the front. They displayed their goods so the customers could see them. The shelves were full of all kinds of products. There were even fancy shawls, pretty china cups and saucers, fine writing paper, and dried figs and raisins.

Missouri towns were full of different kinds of people. There were Kentucky hunters dressed in deerskin and carrying rifles. They shopped along with French people dressed in brightly colored clothes. There were also black slaves doing all sorts of chores for their masters. Boatmen played cards and drank whiskey down by the river while waiting to begin another trip. Native Americans came to town to sell fresh game. Businesspeople made deals, while children played hide-and-seek along the busy streets. French words could still be heard, but most people now spoke English.

The best lands along the Mississippi River were soon taken. More and more newcomers settled along the Missouri River. Towns like Franklin and Boonville were built in central Missouri. Missouri's new settlers came from all parts of the United States. But most of them came from the southern states. Kentucky, Tennessee, Virginia, and North Carolina sent the most settlers to Missouri. Some of the newcomers were black slaves. They had been forced to leave their homes and families and come to Missouri with their masters. They joined the many African-Americans already living in Missouri.

MISSOURI BECOMES A STATE

Missourians wanted the Missouri Territory to become a state in the United States. Citizens of a state had more freedom to govern themselves than citizens of a territory. Missourians asked the United States Congress to make them a state. Each state had to decide if it would allow its people to own slaves. Missourians asked for their state to be a slave state.

FAMOUS MISSOURIANS

Permission to reproduce
courtesy of Lindenwood
College

Mary Easton Sibley

When she was thirteen years old, Mary Easton moved with her family to St. Louis. St. Louis was still a frontier town. Missouri had not yet become a state. Her father, Rufus Easton, was an early Missouri leader. He wanted Mary to go to school. But there were no schools for girls in St. Louis. Easton sent his daughter to a school in Kentucky. Later Mary married George C. Sibley. Sibley ran the United States government's Indian trading po at Fort Osage in Jackson County.

Fort Osage was on the Missouri River. It was many miles from the nearest settlement. Mary tra eled to Fort Osage on a keelboat. The trip was lor

The Southern states were slave states. The Northern states were free states. The free states did not allow people to own slaves. When Missouri attempted to become a state there were already eleven slave states and eleven free states. The members of Congress from the South wanted Missouri to be admitted as a slave state. Many Northerners did not want any more slave states. Most Missourians, especially the slaveholders, did not want the national government to tell them they could not own slaves. During all of this talk about slavery no one asked the slaves what they wanted. This disagreement over slavery kept Missouri out of the Union for over two years.

Finally, Congress worked out a compromise. Missouri entered the Union as a slave state. Maine also wanted to be a state. It came in as a free state. This agreement meant that there would be twelve slave states and twelve free states in the United States.

and hard. It took a month to get from St. Louis to Fort Osage.

Fort Osage was a busy place. Mary liked her new home. Many famous travelers and explorers stopped at Fort Osage. They could always expect a warm welcome from Mary and George Sibley. Mary often played tunes on her piano for her Indian and white guests. She had brought her piano on a keelboat all the way from St. Louis.

Later the Sibleys moved to St. Charles. Mary Sibley knew there were few schools for young women in Missouri. Many schools allowed boys to attend, but not girls. Mary thought girls should have the same chance to learn as boys.

Mary Sibley began to hold classes in her home. The little school grew. It became a college, and she named it Lindenwood. Today the Lindenwood Colleges in St. Charles are open to both women and men.

Congress also decided to keep slavery out of all the northern parts of the Louisiana Territory except Missouri. This agreement was called the Missouri Compromise.

MISSOURI GETS A CONSTITUTION

Missourians had to write a constitution for their new state. A constitution is an important document. It explains the kind of government the people will have. The voters of Missouri elected a group of people to write the state's first constitution in 1820.

Missouri's first constitution had a bill of rights to protect the people's rights. A bill of rights protects such things as freedom of religion, freedom of speech, freedom of the press, and the right to have a jury trial.

Alexander McNair was Missouri's first governor.

Missouri Historical Society

Missouri's first state government was organized much like it is today. The constitution provided for a legislature to make the state's laws. It was called the General Assembly. The constitution provided for a governor to carry out the state's laws. It also provided for courts to decide what the laws mean and to help settle disputes.

The 1820 Missouri constitution called for the state to establish public schools and build roads. Some things in the first Missouri Constitution were different from what we have today. It allowed only white men to vote. Women could not vote. Black people could not vote. That was not surprising. The state's first constitution said there could be slavery in Missouri.

The voters elected Alexander McNair to be Missouri's first governor. When Congress accepted Missouri's new constitution in 1821, Missouri became the twenty-fourth state to join the Union.

MISSOURI'S CAPITAL CITIES

Missouri's new constitution said that the state capital should be located on the Missouri River near the center of the state. That would make it easier for people in all parts of the state to travel to the capital city. But there was no city at that location in 1821.

Missouri's leaders selected St. Charles to be the state capital until a new capital city could be built in central Missouri. St. Charles was an early Missouri settlement located on the Missouri River not far from where that river flows into the Mississippi. For many years St. Charles had been a frontier outpost. Most of its people had been hunters and traders. Many of Missouri's new American settlers passed through St. Charles on their way to central Missouri.

When Missouri became a state, St. Charles was a growing town. There were several new brick buildings along Main Street. One of them served as Missouri's first state capitol. Governor McNair and the General Assembly met there. The state of Missouri has restored that important building. It is now a state historic site.

The state officials decided to build the new state capital at Jefferson City. They named the state's new capital city for Thomas Jefferson. He had been president at the time of the Louisiana Purchase.

Jefferson City was ready in 1826. The state government moved there from St. Charles in that year. It is a very beautiful capital city. Compare the photographs on page xvi of Missouri's first capitol building in St. Charles and today's capitol building in Jefferson City. Why do you think they are so different?

🖙 New Words

coastline	power	ceremony
newcomer	flatboat	boatmen
compromise	government	colony
constitution	governor	General Assembly

Testing Yourself

1. Why was the Louisiana Purchase important in Missouri history?
2. What three flags flew over early Missouri?
3. Why did American settlers come to Missouri when it belonged to Spain?
4. From what states did most of Missouri's settlers come?
5. Why did Missourians move their capital city to the center of the state?

 Matching Partners

Match the right partners on a separate sheet of paper.

1. George Washington
2. Alexander McNair
3. Thomas Jefferson
4. Meriwether Lewis

a. wrote the Declaration of Independence
b. first president of the United States
c. first governor of the state of Missouri
d. famous American explorer

 Things to Talk About

1. If you had been a French settler in Missouri, what would you have thought about the Louisiana Purchase?
2. Why is a bill of rights important?
3. Have you ever been to Jefferson City? If you have, tell about some of the things you saw there.

✏️ Things to Do

1. Locate the Louisiana Purchase on a map. How many other states can you name that were made out of the Louisiana Purchase?

2. Pretend that you traveled with Lewis and Clark to the Pacific. Write a paper describing some of the things you might have seen and done. Tell what you think you would have liked most about your trip. Tell what you think you would not have liked about your trip.

3. On another sheet of paper, put these items in the order they happened. Look at the time line on this page if you need help.
   Declaration of Independence is written
   Missouri becomes a state
   Louisiana is bought by the United States
   France loses Louisiana to Spain

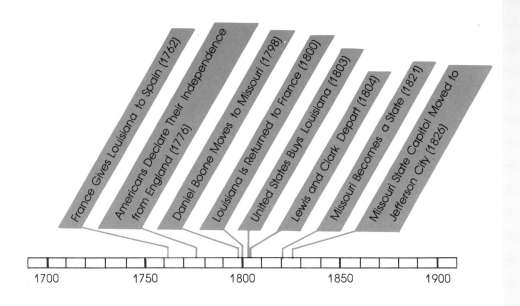

France Gives Louisiana to Spain (1762)
Americans Declare Their Independence from England (1776)
Daniel Boone Moves to Missouri (1798)
Louisiana Is Returned to France (1800)
United States Buys Louisiana (1803)
Lewis and Clark Depart (1804)
Missouri Becomes a State (1821)
Missouri State Capitol Moved to Jefferson City (1826)

1700   1750   1800   1850   1900

Books You Can Read

Barry, James P. *The Louisiana Purchase: Thomas Jefferson Doubles the Area of the United States*. New York: Franklin Watts, 1973.

Blumberg, Rhoda. *The Incredible Journey of Lewis and Clark*. New York: Lothrop, Lee and Shepard, 1987.

Brown, Marion Marsh. *Sacagawea: Indian Interpreter to Lewis and Clark*. Chicago: Childrens Press, 1988.

Chidsey, Donald Barr. *Lewis and Clark: The Great Adventure*. New York: Crown Publishers, 1970.

DeGering, Etta. *Wilderness Way: The Story of Rebecca Bryan Boone*. New York: McKay, 1966.

Gleiter, Jan, and Kathleen Thompson. *Daniel Boone*. Milwaukee: Raintree Childrens Books, 1985.

Greene, Carol. *Daniel Boone: Man of the Forests*. Chicago: Childrens Press, 1990.

Hargrove, Jim. *Daniel Boone: Pioneer Trailblazer*. Chicago: Childrens Press, 1985.

Ingraham, Leonard. *Album of the American Revolution*. New York: Franklin Watts, 1971.

Kent, Zackary. *George Washington: First President of the United States*. Chicago: Childrens Press, 1986.

McGrath, Patrick. *The Lewis and Clark Expedition*. Morristown, N.J.: Silver Burdett, 1985.

Petersen, David, and Mark Coburn. *Meriwether Lewis and William Clark: Soldiers, Explorers, and Partners in History*. Chicago: Childrens Press, 1988.

Phelan, Mary Kay. *The Story of the Louisiana Purchase*. New York: Thomas Y. Crowell, 1979.

Wilkie, Katharine E. *Daniel Boone: Taming the Wilds*. New York: Chelsea House, 1991.

Chapter 6

LIFE ON THE FRONTIER

Find the answers to these questions as you read.

How was pioneer life different from life today?

How did pioneer children learn their lessons?

What did people on the frontier do for fun?

The frontier was at the edge of settlement. It was a place with few people. Most things on the frontier were plain. People had to work hard to survive. Land was cheap. Many people moved to the frontier to make a new start. As more people came and filled up an area, the frontier moved farther west.

PIONEER FARMERS IN MISSOURI

In the early 1800s, Missouri was on the edge of the American frontier. Many settlers wanted to come to Missouri. The soil was rich. Crops grew well. There was plenty of water and timber. Settlers wrote to tell their relatives and friends back home that Missouri was a good land. The word about Missouri spread fast. The number of new settlers coming to Missouri increased. Many of them chose to live close to people from their old neighborhoods.

Many pioneer Missouri families lived in cabins like this one. What kinds of things are the people in the picture doing?

State Historical Society of Missouri

The first pioneers looked for good land with timber. They believed that land with trees growing on it would be good for raising crops. It took hard work to build a farm on the frontier. Often the new settlers brought only a gun, an ax, a few tools, a trunk or chest, and some food and supplies.

Once they had selected the place for their farm, they began cutting down trees. They used the logs to build a cabin. The American pioneers laid the logs lengthwise. They cut notches in the logs so they would not have to use nails to hold them together. Sometimes they joined two separate cabins with a connecting roof. This two-room building was known as a dogtrot cabin. The covered breezeway between the cabins was a cool place in the summer.

Most cabins looked rough and unfinished on the inside. Many had dirt floors. Dogs and hogs sometimes came in from the outside through an open door. The furniture was mostly homemade. The pioneers made their tables from split logs. They used three-legged stools for chairs and straw mattresses for beds. Some fam-

The covered breezeway in the dogtrot cabin was cooler than inside the cabin during the summer.

ilies had a trunk for storing things. A few pioneers brought one or two pieces of good furniture with them. Those items were usually family heirlooms.

The most important place in a frontier log cabin was the fireplace. Almost every cabin had one. It provided heat in winter and was also used for cooking.

Once they had a place to live, the frontier settlers planted crops in the spaces they had cleared. For the first few years, the seeds had to be planted around tree stumps and roots. They used wooden plows to break the earth. The ground was very tough.

Most American farmers raised corn. It grew well. They could make it into corn bread, hominy, and even whiskey. They could store it. They could also feed it to their animals.

Most pioneer families had a few head of livestock. They used oxen and horses for plowing and transportation. Cows supplied milk and butter. The cattle and hogs they raised for meat often ran wild in the woods.

Frontier farms had to produce almost everything the pioneer family needed. These plain people had little or no money to spend. Besides there were no stores nearby. They had to grow enough food for the winter. There were several ways to keep food from spoiling. Fruits and vegetables were dried. Meat was cured with salt. The pioneers hunted deer, bear, turkey, and other wild game. They also gathered wild fruits and fished. They made their own maple sugar and salt.

All family members worked. Women often joined the men in the fields. The women also made most of the family clothing. They grew cotton and flax, and they raised sheep for wool. The American pioneers spun these fibers into thread with a spinning wheel. They then wove the thread into cloth on a hand loom.

Children had regular chores to do. They worked in the garden, gathered wood for the fireplace, took care of the farm animals, milked the cows, and helped harvest the crops. The whole family helped make candles and soap from animal fat.

Life was often very lonely on the frontier. This was especially true for women. There were few close neighbors. Sometimes the closest people were Indians. Often the pioneer settlers remained on friendly terms with the nearby Native Americans. Their children sometimes played together in the woods. Occasionally the men even hunted together. In many ways their lives were similar. Both the Indian people and their pioneer neighbors hunted, fished, gathered wild food, and farmed. The Indian women and the white women turned corn into meal cakes and deer meat into dried venison.

When too many settlers moved onto their lands, the Native Americans became angry. Indian people and white settlers fought over the land. Sometimes they killed each other in battles.

A PIONEER MISSOURI FAMILY

The Coles were a pioneer family in central Missouri. William Temple and Hannah Cole and their nine children moved from

Virginia to Kentucky. They next moved from Kentucky to Missouri. Stephen and Phoebe Cole and their five children came with them. William and Stephen were brothers, and Hannah and Phoebe were sisters.

After they got to Missouri, the Coles camped with some other pioneers on an island in the Missouri River near Hermann. While they were there, a band of Indians stole their horses. The men went looking for their missing horses. The Indians attacked them. They killed William Cole and wounded Stephen Cole.

Stephen Cole recovered from his wounds. Stephen, Phoebe, Hannah, and their children decided to travel farther up the Missouri River. They chose a place near Boonville to settle. The Coles were the first white settlers in that area. Hannah and her children drove their only cow through the woods to Boonville so they would have milk.

They arrived during the winter months. They camped out in a tent. The Missouri River was full of ice. They could not get across the river. They almost ran out of food. They ate acorns, tree bark, and a wild turkey they killed. Then they got some more food from settlers on the other side of the river.

Hannah Cole and her children built a cabin at Boonville. For two years Stephen and Phoebe and their children were Hannah's only neighbors. They lived more than a mile away. Then other families settled nearby. The Coles ate mostly wild meat, milk, corn bread, and honey during their first years at Boonville.

The dangers of the frontier did not stop Hannah. She and her new neighbors built a log fort on her land. They called it Hannah's Fort. Many settlers came there when there was trouble with the Indians.

Hannah Cole's cabin became a meeting place for settlers in the area. Church services were held there. At different times her cabin was used as a school, a post office, and a place to vote on election day.

Hannah Cole was also a businesswoman. She bought and sold much of the land in the Boonville area. When Hannah's Fort was first built, settlers often had to swim across the Missouri River. There

Many frontier schools were one-room log cabins.

State Historical Society of Missouri

was no boat for crossing. Hannah Cole and her sons decided to start a ferryboat service. This was the first ferry across the Missouri River at Boonville.

FRONTIER SCHOOLS

The pioneers first built their homes and planted their crops. Then they began to think about schools. Women worked hard to start schools. They wanted their children to learn.

Americans believed schools were important. They wanted to have a country run by the people. This is a called a democracy. If a country is run by the people, the people need to be able to make wise decisions. Schools help make better citizens.

Starting a school on the frontier was not easy. At first there were only a few families. They lived far apart. They could not send their children to the same school.

Soon there were enough children to start a school. Early schools were very different from our schools today. Many of the first schoolhouses were one-room log cabins. Some had dirt floors. The children sat on log benches. These benches were made by splitting a tree trunk. They were not very comfortable.

In frontier days the teacher was usually a man. Lessons were recited aloud. Students of all ages attended class in the same room. Often students had to leave school for several months each year to help on the farms.

FRONTIER CHURCHES

Many American settlers lived too far apart to have a church. Traveling ministers, called circuit riders, visited small settlements without churches.

The circuit riders sometimes walked, but usually they rode horses. Many times they traveled alone. They stayed overnight with pioneer families. Circuit riders preached any place they could. They held services in barns, courthouses, and even taverns. If there was no large building, the meetings were held outside.

Camp meetings were large outdoor religious meetings. People

Traveling ministers, called circuit riders, visited small settlements without churches.

State Historical Society of Missouri

FAMOUS MISSOURIANS

Saint Rose Philippine Duchesne

Missouri Historical Society

A Catholic nun was sitting at a table writing a letter. It was so cold that the ink froze in the tip of the quill pen she was using. The water in a bucket also had frozen. So had the clothes she had hung out to dry beside the small stove in the log cabin where she lived. The cabin's doors and windows did not close tight.

Mother Rose Philippine Duchesne was in St. Charles, Missouri. She had come from France with four other Catholic sisters to start a school for girls. Life on the frontier was hard for these French women. During their first winter in America the only foods they could get were corn, salt pork, and potatoes. They could not buy eggs, butter, oil, fruit, or vegetables in St. Charles. Mother Duchesne and the other nuns did much of the

came from miles around. Sometimes there were many preachers. Families camped out at the meeting place in tents and would stay for several days. There was much preaching and singing. Women, men, and children, white and black, worshiped together. They also had a chance to visit with the other people who came to the camp meeting.

Once more settlers moved into the area, they organized congregations and built church buildings. Women were often very involved in church activities. They taught Sunday school classes. They also raised money to help people.

work themselves. They raised their own food and took care of their cattle.

St. Charles was not the best place for their school at the time. It was too far from Missouri's other settlements to get enough students. After one year, Mother Duchesne moved the school to Florissant. Later she started another school in St. Louis. Most of the girls had to pay to attend classes. But the Catholic sisters also operated free schools for poor girls who could not afford to pay.

There were not many schools for girls on the frontier. Many people felt that women did not need to go to school. Mother Duchesne hoped to change that. She helped start many schools in America. Before she died, she had set up schools for white, black, and Indian children. Because of her work, many frontier children had their first chance to go to school.

In 1988 the Catholic Church made Mother Rose Philippine Duchesne a saint. She was only the fifth person in the United States to become a Catholic saint.

FUN ON THE FRONTIER

In early Missouri there were no parks, theaters, shopping malls, or sports stadiums. There were no televisions or video games for entertainment. Frontier settlers spent most of their time working on their farms. One's closest neighbor might live several miles away. Roads were bad. Neighbors did not see each other very often.

When they did get together, it was usually to help one another. Settlers found that by working together they could finish a job much quicker. There was a spirit of cooperation on the frontier.

Settlers came from miles around for a camp meeting. It was not unusual for people to stay several days.

Bethel Baptist Church near Cape Girardeau was an early Missouri church building.

Neighbors often gathered to help build a new house or barn.

State Historical Society of Missouri

Whenever a neighbor needed help, it was a reason for a party. The marriage of a young couple was a time to have a house raising. Neighbors from miles around gathered to build the couple a new cabin or barn. Almost every farmer grew corn. When the corn was picked and ready to husk, the settlers had a corn-husking bee. Anyone who found a red ear of corn could kiss someone they liked. Quilting bees were popular with the women and girls. It took many weeks or months for one person to sew a quilt. Working together, the women could finish one in a few days.

There were more things to do in frontier towns. People sometimes met to hear a speaker. They enjoyed good public speaking. Many of the best speakers were politicians running for office.

The Fourth of July was a special holiday. Americans celebrated the signing of the Declaration of Independence with picnics, horse races, contests, and parades. Men fired their guns in honor

At a husking bee, the lucky person who found a red ear of corn could ask for a kiss.

State Historical Society of Missouri

of the day.

Many Missourians also liked to read. Frontier stores in Missouri usually sold books, but some pioneers were too poor to buy them. Books were prized possessions. There were no books in some homes. In others the Bible was the only book. Some people living in towns started libraries. They knew that reading was an easy way to learn new things. However, many Missouri pioneers never learned to read.

THE OZARKS FRONTIER

Missouri's hilly Ozarks region attracted a different kind of pioneer. The thin rocky soil was not good for raising crops. The steep hills made it more difficult to travel in the Ozarks. Fewer settlers came there.

The pioneers who did settle in the Ozarks came mostly from the hill country of Kentucky and Tennessee. The Ozarks reminded them of their former homes. They knew about living in that kind of country. They were mostly hunters and trappers. They lived in plain log cabins. Hunting and fishing were their main activities.

The Ozarks pioneers planted small corn patches, but most of them did not have a vegetable garden. They ate mostly corn bread, wild game, and fish. It was not an easy life, but they loved the beautiful Ozarks woods and streams. For them, it was the best kind of life.

The United States government moved several Indian tribes from the eastern states into the empty areas of the Ozarks. The Delaware, Shawnee, Kickapoo, and Piankashaw Indians settled in the Gasconade, Jacks Fork, and James river valleys. Later those tribes had to move farther west.

 ## New Words

frontier	loom	election
heirloom	democracy	ferry
plow	quilt	nun

 ## Testing Yourself

1. Why did people want to move to Missouri?

2. What tools did pioneers bring with them to the frontier?

3. What kinds of food did the pioneers eat?

4. How did settlers keep their food from spoiling?

5. How did pioneer settlers sometimes help their neighbors?

6. Why did fewer settlers move into the Ozarks?

Things to Do

1. Pretend you are a pioneer in the early days. You and your family are going to Missouri to clear a farm and build a log cabin. Below are several things that you might like to take with you. Choose six things that you would be able to use. Write them on a separate sheet of paper.

toaster	seed	spinning wheel
gun	cow	plow
dishwasher	ax	radio

2. The best pioneer schools did not have many of the things found in today's schools. Five of the things below would not have been found in a pioneer school. Find them and write them down on a separate sheet of paper.

candles	electric clock
motion picture projector	table
books	fire alarm
drinking fountain	gymnasium
fireplace	computer

 # Things to Talk About

1. How is your school different from a pioneer school?
2. Talk about the way a pioneer family made its clothing.
3. Suppose that you and your family had come to early Missouri to start a new farm. Which jobs might be yours?
4. Why was corn a good frontier crop?

5. Why is it important to have good schools in a democracy?

6. If you had been Hannah Cole, would you have stayed on the frontier? Why?

 Books You Can Read

Brenner, Barbara. *On the Frontier with Mr. Audubon*. New York: Coward, McCann, and Geoghegan, 1977.

Hubbard, Margaret A. *Dear Philippine: The Mission of Mother Duchesne*. New York: Farrar, Straus and Giroux, 1964.

Lazarus, Lois. *With These Hands They Built a New Nation: The Story of Colonial Arts and Crafts*. New York: Julian Messner, 1971.

McCall, Edith. *Pioneer Traders*. Chicago: Childrens Press, 1964.

Schaeffer, Elizabeth. *Dandelion, Pokeweed, and Goosefoot*. Reading, Mass.: Addison-Wesley, 1972

Tunis, Edwin. *Frontier Living*. Cleveland: World, 1976.

Wooldridge, Rhoda. *Hannah's Brave Years*. New York: Bobbs-Merrill, 1964. (Fiction)

Wright, Louis B. *Everyday Life on the American Frontier*. New York: Putnam's, 1968.

Chapter 7

EARLY TRAVEL

Find the answers to these questions as you read.

Why did early Missourians travel more on water than on land?

How were flatboats and keelboats different?

What were the first roads like?

Imagine what your life would be like without automobiles, trucks, trains, or airplanes. Early Missourians had none of them. They could not travel or transport goods as easily as we do today.

MISSOURI'S FIRST HIGHWAYS

Rivers were the first highways in Missouri. Indian people usually traveled along the rivers. There were no roads as we know them. There were only a few trails through the forests.

The European explorers and the pioneer settlers traveled by water when they could. River travel was faster than overland travel. The early roads were often only poorly marked trails. It was easy for a traveler who did not know the way to become lost. Cross-country travelers had to make their way through forests filled with trees, vines, and brush. They also had to cross rivers and streams. There were no bridges or ferries. Often there was no place for travelers to spend the night. They had to sleep on the ground. It is easy to see why most people preferred traveling by boat rather than on horseback or by wagon.

There were also problems with river travel. River conditions sometimes forced travelers to delay their trips. During the winter frozen rivers and ice jams made travel by water difficult or impossible. Spring floods could also make the water too risky for boats. At other times low water caused by a lack of rain made boat travel unsafe.

Swift currents, floating logs, and snags were always a danger. They frequently caused boats to overturn and sink. River navigation took skill, and travelers always had to be on the lookout for trouble.

FLATBOATS AND KEELBOATS

Missouri's early settlers used many different kinds of boats. At first, they used Indian canoes and dugouts. These boats were better for travel than for shipping goods.

Missourians began to grow more grains and farm produce than they needed for their families. To sell their extra products, the farmers had to get them to places where people would buy them. New Orleans was such a place. It was located at the mouth of the Mississippi River. Ships from all over the world docked at New Orleans to buy and sell products.

Missourians needed a way to move their produce to New Orleans. Canoes and dugouts were too small for moving the bulky Missouri products to New Orleans.

Flatboats could carry large loads and float easily down the river. Getting a flatboat upstream was a different matter. Often the owners of flatboats sold them in New Orleans for firewood. It was

Flatboats floated down the river loaded with grain, meat, cheese, and other products.

Moving a keelboat upstream was not an easy chore. Notice that some of the men on the boat are using poles and other men are walking along the bank pulling the boat with a cordelle rope.

too much work to haul them back up the river.

The keelboat began to replace the flatboat. The keelboat could go both upstream and downstream. It was stronger than a flatboat, but moving a keelboat upstream was not an easy chore. River currents were strong. Sometimes the people on one side of a keelboat would row with oars. Those on the other side would grab the bushes along the bank and pull the boat forward.

Frequently a rope was fastened to the keelboat's mast, and the crew walked along the riverbank pulling the boat. This was called "cordelling." At other times the crew used long poles. They placed them on the river bottom and pushed the boat up the river. If there was a strong wind blowing in the right direction, the crew put up the boat's sail and let the breeze push the boat along. For many years, keelboats were the best way to travel up the rivers.

THE STEAMBOAT

The invention of the steamboat was a very important development for Missourians. The steamboat had a powerful steam engine. The engine turned the great paddle wheels that pushed the boat through the water. Steamboats were larger than flatboats or keelboats. They could carry more passengers and larger loads. They moved faster and traveled upstream without any problem.

The steamboats brought many changes to Missouri. They transported more new settlers to the state. They made it easier for Missourians to trade with other places. Steamboats hauled Missouri wheat, livestock, cotton, hemp, and lead to distant markets. They brought goods from all parts of the world to the state.

At first the steamboats operated only on the state's two largest rivers, the Mississippi and the Missouri. Business activity increased in river cities like St. Louis, Hannibal, Jefferson City, Glasgow, Lexington, Westport Landing, Weston, and St. Joseph. Later steamboats traveled on the smaller Osage, Gasconade, and White rivers.

The day the steamboat came to town was an exciting one. The

FAMOUS MISSOURIANS

Samuel L. Clemens

It was a hot summer afternoon. The river town of Hannibal, Missouri, was quiet and peaceful. Suddenly a steamboat whistle sounded in the distance. Then someone shouted, "Steamboat a-comin!" All at once, the town came to life. Everyone ran toward the docks along the riverbank. Workers began moving huge bales and heavy barrels. The steamboat was coming closer. The peopl along the banks could hear the giant paddle wheels splash through the water. Smoke poured from the boat's two tall smokestacks.

A small group of children had gathered nearby to watch the excitement. One of them was Samuel Clemens. Sam loved the river. His greatest wish was to become a riverboat pilot.

Sam Clemens was born in Florida, Missouri, bu he grew up in Hannibal. When his father died, h had to go to work. His family was very poor. At the age of twelve, Sam got a job working for a newspaper in Hannibal. He worked hard. Soon h had learned to be a good printer.

Sam Clemens wanted to see new places, and he left Hannibal. He traveled to New York and Phila

people first saw the tall smokestacks. Before long they heard the sounds of the loud steam whistle and the splashing paddle wheel. When someone spotted a steamboat, they shouted "Steamboat a-comin." A crowd would quickly gather at the river. Some people

delphia, but he came back to the Mississippi. He still wanted to be a riverboat pilot. Clemens learned quickly. Soon he received his pilot's license. He piloted steamboats up and down the Mississippi River.

Then the Civil War came. Times were bad, and Clemens lost his job. He decided to go west with his brother. They went to the Nevada Territory in a stagecoach.

When Clemens got to Nevada, he tried his luck looking for gold. He did not strike it rich, but the other miners liked the funny stories he told. Clemens went to work for a newspaper in Virginia City, Nevada. He began writing stories. Clemens soon became a famous writer.

Clemens wrote books under the name *Mark Twain*. He borrowed his name from his days as a riverboat pilot. As a steamboat traveled along the river, the boatman would call out, "By the mark, twain!" This meant that the water was deep enough for the boat to go ahead safely.

Clemens never returned to Missouri to live. But he wrote about Hannibal and his days as a Mississippi River steamboat pilot. *The Adventures of Tom Sawyer, Adventures of Huckleberry Finn*, and *Life on the Mississippi* are all based upon his life in Missouri.

came to help with the loading and unloading. Others came just to watch the activity.

Steamboats were beautiful and graceful. People who built and owned the boats were very proud of them. They often bragged

When the steamboat came into town, people gathered to watch the boat dock. At what city in Missouri do you think this boat has stopped?

Steamboats were beautiful and graceful.

that their boats were the biggest, fastest, and fanciest on the river.

A steamboat trip was exciting. Wealthy people rode in beautiful rooms with fancy furniture. They dined on fine food and drink. Those with less money traveled on the open deck. They often carried their own food with them.

The steamboat pilot had an important and exciting job. He kept the steamboat in the deepest part of the river. Both the Missouri and the Mississippi rivers were filled with hidden dangers. A pilot had to know where the snags and sandbars were. He needed to know how fast the current was in each part of the river.

Steamboat accidents were always a danger. A hidden log in the river could cause a boat to sink. If the boiler in the engine became too hot, it would explode. A boiler explosion on the steamboat *Saluda* killed over one hundred people in Missouri.

EARLY ROADS

Travel on land was very difficult in frontier Missouri. The early settlers cleared a few short dirt roads. These roads usually connected a settlement with a nearby river. When people began settling away from the rivers, they needed more and better roads.

Road building was slow and expensive. Sometimes neighbors formed "road bees" to work on roads. This gave them a chance to visit and hear the latest news. Every man in the community was expected to work on the roads.

Still, most early roads were poorly built. They were rough. After a heavy rain they were muddy. Road builders cut down trees, but they left stumps in the roadway just low enough for a wagon to pass over. It was difficult to travel or haul goods over these roads.

Missourians looked for better ways to build roads. One thing they tried was the plank road. They placed wooden planks crosswise over the roadbed. The plank roads were smooth until it rained or snowed a few times. The water caused the boards to warp and rot. This soon made them too bumpy to use.

Plank roads soon became bumpy.

Library of Congress

THE RAILROAD

Railroads were another new form of transportation. They had many advantages. Steam power allowed a railroad engine to pull many cars over a set of tracks. Railroad tracks could be laid almost anywhere. This made it possible to provide transportation in parts of the state where there were no rivers. Railroads could operate in most kinds of weather. Rail cars could carry much more than freight wagons. Trains traveled at higher speeds and were more comfortable for passengers than wagons or stage-coaches.

Railroads greatly improved transportation in Missouri, but they were expensive to build. The Hannibal and St. Joseph was an early railroad. It connected those two Missouri cities. The Pacific Railroad operated between St. Louis and Sedalia before the Civil War. But the greatest changes involving railroads were yet to come.

Railroads greatly improved transportation in Missouri.

State Historical Society of Missouri

 # New Words

current	upstream	steamboat
dugout	keelboat	boiler
warp	snag	sandbar

 # Testing Yourself

1. What kinds of travel do we have today that early Missourians did not have?

2. Why were the rivers important to early Missourians?

3. What were some of the dangers of river travel in early Missouri?

4. Name the different kinds of boats early Missourians used.

5. How was a keelboat better than a flatboat?

6. How was a steamboat better than a flatboat or a keelboat?

7. What were early Missouri roads like?

8. What made railroads a better kind of transportation than river travel?

Choose the Right Words

Select the right words to complete each of the following statements. Then write the entire sentence correctly on another sheet of paper.

1. Indian people in Missouri mainly depended upon (river, land) travel.

2. The earliest settlers depended mostly upon (river, land) travel.

3. Boat crews sometimes moved a (keelboat, steamboat) by pulling it with a rope as they walked along the riverbank.

4. Of the different kinds of water travel, the (flatboat, steamboat) brought the most changes to Missouri.

5. The (pilot, engineer) had the most important job on a steamboat.

6. Early Missourians traveled over land roads in (wagons, automobiles).

7. Many early Missouri roads were built by ("road bees," construction companies).

 # Things to Talk About

1. Would you have liked to travel on a steamboat? Why or why not?

2. Pretend you live in early Missouri. Your family is visiting friends in another community. How is your trip different from one a family might take today?

3. Pretend you are a steamboat pilot on the Missouri River. What are some of the things you would be looking out for?

Books You Can Read

Beales, Joan. *The True Book of Travel by Land.* Chicago: Childrens Press, 1968.

Kane, Harnett T. *Young Mark Twain and the Mississippi.* New York: Random House, 1966.

McCague, James. *Flatboat Days on the Frontier Rivers.* Champaign, Ill.: Garrard, 1968.

McCall, Edith. *Men on Iron Horses.* Chicago: Childrens Press, 1980.

————. *Mississippi Steamboatman: The Story of Henry Miller Schreve.* New York: Walter and Co., 1985.

————. *Steamboats to the West.* Chicago: Childrens Press, 1980.

North, Sterling. *Mark Twain and the River.* Boston: Houghton-Mifflin, 1961.

Stein, R. Conrad. *The Story of the Mississippi Steamboats.* Chicago: Childrens Press, 1987.

Chapter 8

MISSOURI AND THE WEST

Find the answers to these questions as you read.

Why did so many settlers decide to move west?

Why was Missouri called the Gateway to the West?

How did people travel the long way to the West?

Today Missouri is in the central part of the United States. When the first settlers came to Missouri, it was on the edge of the frontier. There was a big land west of Missouri. There were Native Americans, Spaniards, and Mexicans living in some parts of it. But most Americans then believed that the far West was an empty land waiting to be settled.

As time went by, the Americans became more interested in the West. Land in the United States was filling up with farms and cities. It cost more to buy good land. Many people thought that much of the United States was becoming crowded. They began looking for new frontiers to settle. The West seemed to be a place where they could go.

Missouri became the jumping-off place for people traveling west. It also became a warehouse for products from the West.

The Gateway Arch in St. Louis is a beautiful monument to western expansion.

Missouri Division of Tourism

Many famous western explorers and pioneers were women and men from Missouri. Missouri was the Gateway to the West. The Gateway Arch in St. Louis is a beautiful monument to western expansion. The exhibits in the Museum of Westward Expansion under the Gateway Arch help tell the story of Missouri's part in western settlement.

THE FUR TRADE

Lewis and Clark had reported that the Rocky Mountain valleys were filled with beaver and other animals. Businessmen in St. Louis started new companies to trade for furs in the far West. They sent hundreds of trappers to the West. They went to trap animals for

Native Americans came to trading posts to sell furs.

State Historical Society of Missouri

furs and to trade with the Indians for furs.

These trappers traveled up the Missouri River and into the Rocky Mountains. They explored the western lands. They became known as mountain men. The mountain men faced many dangers. They had to watch out for grizzly bears and rattlesnakes. They had to find food and shelter. It was difficult to stay alive in the mountains during winter snows. Sometimes they had to face angry Indians. The Native Americans did not want the mountain men to kill so many animals in their land.

The trappers caught large numbers of beaver, otter, mink, and fox. They also killed many buffalos, bears, and deer. They sent the furs and skins from these animals to the fur companies in St. Louis. Beaver skins were especially valuable. Hatmakers used the beaver fur for making felt hats for men.

The most famous mountain men came from Missouri. Kit Carson, Jim Bridger, James P. Beckwourth, and Jedediah Smith all lived in Missouri at some time. Missouri businessmen like William H. Ashley and Pierre Chouteau, Jr., made fortunes in the fur trade. Ashley was also a successful politician.

The mountain men liked the West. They loved its great natural beauty. They told exciting stories about living in the West. Their tales about the West made other Americans want to go there. Mountain men later served as guides for people traveling west.

THE SANTA FE TRADE

Santa Fe was a Spanish settlement far to the southwest of Missouri. Today it is in the state of New Mexico. There were no other

The Arrow Rock Tavern was a favorite stopping place for travelers on the Santa Fe trail.

Missouri Division of Tourism

FAMOUS MISSOURIANS

James P. Beckwourth

Dictionary of American Portraits; courtesy State Historical Society of Missouri

There were hundreds of mountain men who helped explore the West, but only a few became famous. James P. Beckwourth was America's most famous African-American mountain man. He came to Missouri with his family when he was twelve years old. At first he worked in a St. Louis blacksmith shop. That was not exciting enough for young Jim Beckwourth.

One day he decided to join a group going to the Rocky Mountains to hunt for furs. Beckwourth's first trip in the Rocky Mountains was very diffi-

large settlements near Santa Fe. People who lived there could not get many things they needed. Missouri traders believed that they could make money by selling goods in Santa Fe.

William Becknell made a trading trip to Santa Fe the year that Missouri became a state. He became known as the "Father of the Santa Fe trade." Soon other traders set out for Santa Fe. They loaded their wagons with cotton and woolen cloth, iron pots and pans, tools, knives, and mirrors. They traveled in wagon trains for protection. The Indian people did not like so many strangers crossing their land. But they usually did not attack groups of wagons.

The trip to Santa Fe was long and difficult. Each wagon was pulled by several mules or oxen. The rocky trail often made the animals' feet sore. There was little water along the trail.

The Santa Fe trail was eight hundred miles long. It began in

cult. When winter came, there was not enough food to eat. Some days each trapper got only a half-pint of flour mixed with a little water. The snow was deep. It was hard to find wild game for food.

Beckwourth's first trip was hard. But he went back to the Rockies many more times. For several years he lived and hunted with the Crow Indians. He learned their language and their ways. They made him an honorary chief. Beckwourth was one of the best trappers and fur traders in the American West. He later ran a trading post and owned a hotel.

Beckwourth traveled all over the West. When gold was discovered in California, he went there. He guided many wagon trains to California since he knew the West so well. He even started a new road to California. Beckwourth also worked for the United States Army as a scout and guide.

Franklin, Missouri. Arrow Rock became a favorite stopping place for travelers on the Santa Fe trail. Many of them stayed at the Arrow Rock Tavern. The tavern still serves meals to visitors. It is a state historic site. Independence later replaced Franklin as the starting place for the Santa Fe trail. Independence was closer to Santa Fe. The Santa Fe trail made Independence an important jumping-off place for Americans traveling west. Today the National Frontier Trails Center museum is located in Independence.

In Santa Fe the traders swapped their goods for furs, horses, burros, mules, and silver. The goods they brought back to Missouri were usually worth more than the goods that they had taken there. That meant they earned a profit.

Missourians became famous for raising mules. The animals brought from Santa Fe helped the state's mule business. Mis-

This is how Independence looked when many people were traveling through on their way to the far West.

sourians used mules as work animals. They also sold them to buyers in other states. The Missouri mule became one of the state's symbols.

A MISSOURI BOY GOES WEST

Christopher "Kit" Carson was an important western pioneer. His family moved to Missouri when he was very young. When Kit was fourteen years old, he went to work as a saddlemaker's apprentice in Franklin, Missouri. Kit did not like his job. He ran away to Independence, Missouri.

Independence was a busy place. Traders there told exciting stories about Santa Fe. Kit decided to join a wagon train to find out about Santa Fe for himself. Kit's master was not happy that his young worker had run away. He put an advertisement in the Franklin newspaper. He offered a one-cent reward for the boy's return. No one ever collected the reward. Kit Carson had begun a new life.

THE WEST IN 1850

CANADA

Columbia River

Oregon Territory

ROCKY

Mississippi River

Missouri River

Platte River

GREAT

St. Joseph

MOUNTAINS

Independence

Missouri

California

PLAINS

Santa Fe

Texas

Austin

———— Oregon Trail
- - - - Santa Fe Trail
∼∼∼∼∼∼ California Trail

MEXICO

Carson worked at many different jobs after going west. From other trappers he learned to find beaver. He traveled in many parts of the West. Carson had many narrow escapes. Once, two grizzly bears attacked him. He was able to climb a tree, but he had lost his gun. Carson had to stay there for several hours until the bears went away.

Kit Carson became a famous guide. He knew the West. He also knew and understood the Indian people. He spoke several different Indian languages and also spoke Spanish. Carson led many wagon trains west and served as a guide for the United States Army. He was an Indian agent, too. Later in his career Carson joined the United States Army and became a general. Even today Americans still remember the boy who ran away from Franklin so that he could go west.

AMERICAN SETTLEMENT IN TEXAS

Missourians also played an important part in the American settlement of Texas. Moses Austin was a well-known Missouri lead miner. He got permission from the Spanish government to take several hundred American families into Texas. Moses Austin died before he could settle in Texas. But his son Stephen carried out his plans.

Many Missourians moved to Texas during its early years. Later the Americans who settled in Texas declared their independence from Mexico and formed a new country. They called it the Lone Star Republic. Later Texas became a part of the United States. Today the capital of Texas is Austin. It was named for Stephen Austin.

GOING TO OREGON

The reports of Lewis and Clark and the tales of the mountain men made many people curious about the Oregon country. Lewis and Clark and the mountain men had been among the first Americans to visit this area in the Northwest. A few missionaries also settled in Oregon.

A small number of settlers made the long trip to the Oregon country. They wrote to their friends and families. They reported that the land was rich and there was plenty of rain. They encouraged other Americans to come.

A steady stream of settlers soon began moving to Oregon. Almost all of them began their trip in Missouri. They bought wagons, tools, food, and other supplies for the trip in places like Independence, Westport Landing (now a part of Kansas City), and St. Joseph. This business caused these towns to grow.

The path they followed became known as the Oregon Trail. It was over two thousand miles long. The trail passed through plains and deserts, over mountains, and across rivers.

There were no real roads. There were no bridges. When the rivers were too deep to wade through, the travelers had to swim

Settlers moving west sometimes traveled by water to Westport Landing, where they joined a wagon train.

State Historical Society of Missouri

across with their animals. They floated their wagons across.

In a few years the states of Oregon and Washington were formed out of the Oregon country.

THE CALIFORNIA GOLD RUSH

Gold was discovered in California in 1848. Soon even more people were passing through Missouri. Some Missourians caught the gold fever too. They sold their farms and left their jobs and families to go west. They joined the wagon trains going to California. The gold rush increased business in the western Missouri towns. Each spring they were crowded with people ready to travel west.

The gold in California did not last long, and only a few people struck it rich. But many who went to California decided that it was a good place to live. They stayed there, and others joined them. When California became a state many of its citizens had once lived in Missouri.

Stage coaches carried passengers and mail from Missouri to California.

State Historical Society of Missouri

OVERLAND COMMUNICATION AND TRANSPORTATION

The settlers in the far West wanted faster mail service. Ships carried most mail and supplies from the east around the southern tip of South America. That trip took several months.

John Butterfield organized a company to carry mail between Missouri and California. It was the Butterfield Overland Mail Company. Mail from the east was taken by train to Tipton, where the railroad line ended. From there it was transported all the way to California in horse-drawn stagecoaches. The stagecoaches also carried passengers.

The stage stopped only for meals and to exchange tired horses for fresh ones. Before the stage left Missouri, it made stops at Warsaw, Wheatland, Elkton, Bolivar, Brighton, Springfield, Clever, and Cassville. The trip from Missouri to California took about twenty-five days. People considered that to be a very fast time.

Missourians William B. Russell, Alexander Majors, and W. B. Waddell organized the first company to haul supplies to the new settlements in the Great Plains and the Rocky Mountains. The company's name was Russell, Majors and Waddell. Its headquarters was in Lexington. At one time, the company operated over three thousand wagons. It employed four thousand people and used forty thousand oxen to pull the wagons.

The wagons carried guns, plows, machinery, food products, and other supplies needed to operate the mining camps, farms, ranches, and army posts on the frontier. On the trip back to Missouri, the wagons brought hides, furs, gold, and silver.

THE PONY EXPRESS

Everyone wanted still faster mail service. Russell, Majors, and Waddell started the Pony Express to deliver the mail to California more quickly. The Pony Express riders carried the mail from St. Joseph, Missouri, to Sacramento, California. Skilled riders carrying the mail galloped fast horses across the plains and mountains.

Pony Express riders carried the mail from Missouri to California.

State Historical Society of Missouri

Each year many people visit the old Pony Express stables.

Missouri Division of Tourism

The riders could weigh no more than 125 pounds. Because of this, most of the Pony Express riders were young boys.

A horse could run fast only for a short time. Every fifteen miles the riders changed horses at a company station. It usually took about ten days to carry the mail across the two thousand miles to California. The record trip was seven days.

The Pony Express did not last long. A new telegraph line soon crossed the continent. Messages could be sent across the country over the telegraph wire in a few minutes. The Pony Express was no longer needed.

The Pony Express and its riders have become famous in the story of the West. Each year many people visit the old Pony Express stables in St. Joseph.

New Words

fortune	stagecoach	supplies
mule	gallop	apprentice
stables	profit	

 ## Testing Yourself

1. What Missouri city became the center for the fur trade?
2. What kinds of animal furs and skins did the traders and trappers want?
3. What kinds of things did the Missouri traders take to Santa Fe to trade?
4. What kinds of things did the Missouri traders bring back from Santa Fe?
5. From which Missouri towns did the wagon trains leave as they headed west?
6. Why was the Pony Express started?

 ## Things to Talk About

1. What does it mean to earn a profit? Why is it important for a business to make a profit? Explain how the Santa Fe traders made a profit.
2. Why was it useful for a western explorer like Kit Carson to speak English, Spanish, and several Indian languages? Why is it important today to learn to speak more than one language?

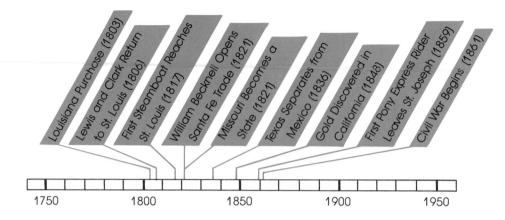

Louisiana Purchase (1803)
Lewis and Clark Return to St. Louis (1806)
First Steamboat Reaches St. Louis (1817)
William Becknell Opens Santa Fe Trade (1821)
Missouri Becomes a State (1821)
Texas Separates from Mexico (1836)
Gold Discovered in California (1848)
First Pony Express Rider Leaves St. Joseph (1859)
Civil War Begins (1861)

1750   1800   1850   1900   1950

✏️ Things to Do

1. Pretend that you are a trader who has just arrived in Santa Fe. Write a letter to a friend describing your trip from Missouri.

2. Make believe that you are in Independence getting ready to travel to California with a wagon train. What would you carry on the trip? What problems would you expect to face on the trip?

3. Select a famous Missourian who helped settle the American West. Write a short paragraph about that person. You might need to visit your library to get more information.

4. Find out how long it would take you today to travel in an automobile or an airplane from Independence to Sacramento.

Describing People

On a separate sheet of paper, write the name of each of the following persons. Then write beside each name the phrase in the second column that best describes each.

1. William Ashley   a. wealthy fur trader

2. James P. Beckwourth   b. a leader in the settlement of Texas

3. William Becknell   c. a famous mountain man

4. Stephen Austin   d. an important Santa Fe trader

 # Books You Can Read

Blassingame, Wyatt. *Jim Beckwourth: Black Trapper and Indian Chief*. Champaign, Ill.: Garrard, 1973.

Dines, Glen. *Bull Wagons, Strong Wheels for Rugged Men: The Frontier Freighters*. New York: MacMillan, 1963.

Glubok, Shirley. *The Art of the Old West*. New York: Macmillan, 1971.

Grant, Matthew. *Kit Carson*. Chicago: Childrens Press, 1974.

Independence, the Queen City of the Trails. Kansas City: Landmark Editions, 1986.

McCall, Edith. *Message from the Mountains*. New York: Walker, 1985. (Fiction)

Montgomery, Elizabeth R. *When Pioneers Pushed West to Oregon*. Champaign, Ill.: Garrard, 1971. (Fiction)

Place, Marian. *The First Book of the Santa Fe Trail*. New York: Franklin Watts, 1966.

Rounds, Glen. *The Prairie Schooners*. New York: Holiday House, 1968.

Stein, R. Conard. *The Story of the Oregon Trail*. Chicago: Childrens Press, 1985.

————. *The Story of the Pony Express*. Chicago: Childrens Press, 1981.

Wooldridge, Rhoda. *Fort Osage: Opening of the American West*. Independence, Mo.: Independence Press, 1983.

Chapter 9

A GROWING STATE

Find the answers to these questions as you read.

How were settlers from the Northern states different from settlers from the Southern states?

Why did immigrants come to America from Europe?

What did the new immigrants give to Missouri?

Who could vote in frontier Missouri?

Missouri grew rapidly after it became a state. New people came to Missouri from many parts of the United States and from Europe. Older cities like St. Louis grew bigger. New cities and towns were established in various parts of the state. Missourians began moving farther away from the rivers. Settlers cleared more land for new farms. Some of Missouri's early pioneer farms had been changed into small plantations. By the time of the American Civil War, Missouri was no longer a frontier state.

Older cities like St. Louis grew rapidly after Missouri became a state.

State Historical Society of Missouri

THE YANKEES COME TO MISSOURI

Before Missouri became a state, most of its American settlers had come from the Southern states. Many had brought slaves with them. Missouri had entered the Union as a slave state. Some new settlers continued to come from the South. But they were joined by more people from the Northern states. These Yankee settlers did not own slaves. Some Northern settlers were farmers. Many others were more interested in business and trade.

WELCOMING NEW IMMIGRANTS TO MISSOURI

Missouri also attracted many new immigrants who came directly from Europe. They came to America for many different reasons. Most were looking for a better life. Some immigrants left their homelands because many people were dying from diseases and a lack of food. Others left to escape from rulers who did not allow them any freedom. Many hoped to become land-owners.

The decision to go to America was never an easy one. It was hard to leave friends and family. The trip across the Atlantic Ocean could be very difficult. But in spite of the hardships, many immigrants came to the United States and to Missouri.

THE GERMANS COME TO MISSOURI

The Germans were the largest group of foreign immigrants that came to Missouri. Gottfried Duden was a German lawyer who wrote a book describing Missouri as a wonderful place to settle. Many Germans read the book and followed Duden to Missouri. Many of the German newcomers settled in St. Louis. Others went to places like Hermann, Westphalia, Washington, Altenberg, and Wittenberg.

Hermann was established by German immigrants before the Civil War.

State Historical Society of Missouri

The Germans constructed sturdy brick and stone buildings. They were good farmers. Their well-built barns and fenced fields were easy to spot. They raised grapes and made wine. They also brewed beer. The Germans were famous for their good food. They introduced such dishes as sausages, sauerbraten, sauerkraut, and stollen (a sweet bread containing fruit and nuts). Missouri's new German settlers also included many skilled craftsmen, musicians, authors, teachers, and clergymen. Many of them had left Germany to gain more freedom. When they came to Missouri they opposed slavery. Many Germans volunteered to fight for the Union during the Civil War.

A GERMAN IMMIGRANT FAMILY IN MISSOURI

Bernhard and Henriette Bruns were German immigrants who came to Missouri looking for a better life. Bernhard was a doctor. His wife, who was called "Jette," had not wanted to leave Germany. But she agreed to go to Missouri with her husband. They settled on a farm in Osage County. They joined with other German immigrants in helping to establish the town of Westphalia.

Pioneer life was hard on the German couple. They were not used to living in the country. Farming was hard work. They had many disappointments caused by such things as bad weather, floods, poor crops, and diseases. Three of their children died from sickness. Jette was lonely and homesick for Germany. She wrote many letters to her family in Germany.

Doctor Bruns was not a good businessman. The Bruns did not have much money. Many of his patients could not afford to pay him.

Jette wanted to leave Westphalia. The Bruns family moved to Jefferson City. Doctor Bruns became interested in politics. He was elected mayor of Jefferson City. The Bruns lived across the street from the state capitol building. They were there when the Civil War began.

Like most Germans, they were for the Union. Doctor Bruns

Dr. Bernhard Bruns was a surgeon in the Union army during the Civil War.

Courtesy Adolf Schroeder

Henriette Bruns found life in Missouri much different than it had been in Germany.

Courtesy Adolf Schroeder

served as a surgeon in the Union Army. Jette was afraid that the Confederate troops would capture Jefferson City and make them move. That did not happen, but their son Heinrich was killed in a Civil War battle. He was also a Union soldier. Not long after that Doctor Bruns died. Jette was left all alone. She still did not have much money. She rented rooms in her home to support herself. Life in Missouri had been difficult for Jette. Her story shows that moving to a new land was often not an easy thing.

IRISH IMMIGRANTS COME TO MISSOURI

The Irish were another important group of immigrants who arrived from Europe. Many Irish people came to keep from starving.

The potato crop had failed in Ireland, and many people there were hungry. Most of the Irish immigrants had been farmers. When the Irish came to America they were too poor to buy land. They had to settle in the cities. Many of the Irish in Missouri settled in St. Louis, Kansas City, and St. Joseph. They worked as laborers. The railroads used many Irish workers.

CHANGES ON THE FARM

Most Missourians were still farmers. But life on Missouri farms was changing from the early pioneer times. Successful farmers had replaced their log cabins with frame and brick houses. The Southerners who had settled in Missouri used their slaves to build handsome plantations. They grew tobacco, hemp, and cotton and raised livestock. Hemp was used for making rope. Many of the new German settlers were grain farmers.

Farming was hard work. But some Missouri farmers now had better farm implements than the pioneer farmers. John Deere's

The reaper was a new farm machine used for cutting wheat.

State Historical Society of Missouri

Kansas City was a growing city in the western part of the state.

State Historical Society of Missouri

steel plow and Cyrus McCormick's grain reaper were two of the new farm machines that a few Missouri farmers owned. The reaper was used for cutting wheat. These new farm implements were pulled by horses and mules.

MISSOURI'S GROWING TOWNS AND CITIES

Missouri's towns and cities were growing. The people went there to get the things they needed. Merchants operated stores in the towns and cities. James Aull was a pioneer Missouri merchant. He opened a store in Lexington four years after Missouri became a state. He later owned stores in Independence, Richmond, and Liberty. Aull sold many things to his customers.

Some of them were made from products that were raised locally. For example, he sold cornmeal made from Missouri corn, flour made from Missouri wheat, vinegar made from Missouri ap-

George Caleb Bingham

Self-portrait by George Caleb Bingham; Saint Louis Art Museum.

A young boy was drawing pictures on the wall of his grandfather's mill. He was always drawing. He drew pictures wherever he could. His uncle thought that he spent too much time drawing pictures and not enough time doing his farm chores. The boy's name was George Caleb Bingham. He became one of America's greatest artists. Today his paintings of frontier life are worth millions of dollars.

George was born in Virginia. When he was seven years old, the Bingham family moved to Franklin, Missouri. Franklin was a frontier town on the Missouri River. As a boy George watched the frontier trappers, traders, and riverboatmen who came to Franklin. He never forgot them. They were the subjects of some of his most famous paintings.

Life in Missouri was hard for the Binghams. George's father got malaria and died. A short time later the town of Franklin was washed away in a great flood. Mary Bingham took George and her other children across the river to a farm she owned near Arrow Rock. She started a school for girls in Arrow Rock. Mary Bingham hired a woman to teach art at her school. The art teacher also taught George, who was the school's janitor.

George Bingham spent much of his time in Arrow Rock. He liked being there better than working on the farm. He went to work for a cabinetmaker. People in Arrow Rock and other nearby towns paid him to paint their portraits. There were no cameras for taking pictures in those days. People who wanted pictures of themselves had to have them painted.

Bingham got smallpox. The disease caused all of

his hair to fall out. He had to wear a wig for the rest of his life. Bingham married three times. He had several children, and most of them died young. Bingham built a two-room brick house in Arrow Rock that you can still visit today. There is a color photograph of it on page x.

Bingham traveled in the United States and later in Europe. He studied the work of other artists. In Philadelphia he saw paintings showing scenes from daily life. He decided that he could paint pictures of life in frontier Missouri. He did paintings of boatmen, trappers, and people going to vote. He also did a painting of the famous American pioneer Daniel Boone.

Bingham was interested in politics. He was elected to the Missouri House of Representatives. During the Civil War he served as the treasurer of Missouri. Bingham owned slaves, but he supported the Union during the Civil War. He was for the Union, but he did not like the way some Union soldiers treated the people of Missouri. He protested when a Union general made people in western Missouri leave their homes during the war. His painting *Order No. Eleven* shows those people being driven from their homes by Union soldiers. Look at the color photograph of that famous painting on page xi.

After his first wife died Bingham left Arrow Rock. He and his family lived in many different places in America and in Europe. He worked hard to sell his paintings. The best ones sold for a few hundred dollars. That was a lot of money then. But today those same paintings have sold for millions of dollars.

Bingham spent his last years in Missouri. He lived in Jefferson City, Columbia, and Kansas City. He was hired to teach art at the University of Missouri. The boy who liked to draw became a famous American painter, but Missourians will always think of him as the Missouri artist.

ples, rope made from Missouri hemp, lumber and furniture made from Missouri trees, and cured Missouri tobacco.

Other goods had to be brought to Missouri from outside the state. Aull sold tools, stoves, farm implements, clothing, paper, books, and many other items. Doctors, lawyers, printers, craftsmen, and other workers also lived and worked in the towns and cities.

MISSOURI'S EARLY FACTORIES

As Missouri grew, so did Missouri's industries. At first most manufacturing was done in the homes. Women spun thread on their spinning wheels and wove cloth on their looms. Men ground corn into meal with a simple horse-powered mill.

The system for making goods began to change. Manufacturing began to move from the home to small workshops. Workers produced wagons, guns, saddles, furniture, barrels, and clothing. They sold these goods to Missourians and to people passing through Missouri on their way to the West.

GOVERNMENT AND POLITICS IN MISSOURI

After Missouri became a state, its white male citizens took an active role in electing the officials to run the state and the country. Remember that women and blacks could not take part in politics and elections. Look at the pictures on pages x and 143. Missourians talked politics with their neighbors. They attended political rallies and listened to political speeches. Election day was always an exciting time. People turned out to vote.

George Caleb Bingham was a painter who lived in Arrow Rock and Kansas City. He became one of America's greatest artists. Some of his most famous paintings were pictures of Missouri politics and elections. Look at the color photograph of his painting

Missourians talked politics with their neighbors.

Painting by George Caleb Bingham, William Rockhill Nelson Gallery of Art, Kansas City, Missouri; courtesy State Historical Society of Missouri

The County Election on page x. Why are there no women in this picture?

Andrew Jackson was a popular political leader in the United States. He believed in democracy. He wanted the people to have something to say about their government. Missourians helped elect him president of the United States. He was called the people's president.

One of Andrew Jackson's strong supporters was Thomas Hart Benton. Benton was a Missourian. He represented Missouri in the United States Senate for thirty years. He was Missouri's first famous Thomas Hart Benton. Many years later his great-nephew, also named Thomas Hart Benton, became a famous painter. You will read more about Thomas Hart Benton the artist in Chapter 18.

Thomas Hart Benton was a United States senator from Missouri for thirty years.

State Historical Society of Missouri

🖝 New Words

plantation	Yankee	immigrant
clergyman	reaper	portrait
foreign	factory	sauerbraten
sauerkraut	stollen	

Testing Yourself

1. What foreign country sent the largest group of immigrants to Missouri?

2. What were some German foods?

3. Why did so many Irish people come to America?

4. What new inventions made farming easier?

5. What Missouri products did Missouri storekeepers sell to their customers?

6. Why was Andrew Jackson called the people's president?

 Things to Talk About

1. What do you think it would be like to move to another country? What problems do you think you might have?

2. How have immigrants helped make Missouri a better place?

3. How were elections in frontier Missouri different from today's elections?

 Things to Do

1. Look at one of George Caleb Bingham's paintings. What things in it look different from today?

2. Find out if your family knows where your ancestors came from. If they do, see if you can learn something about those places.

Books You Can Read

Baker, Betty. *Dunderhead War*. New York: Harper and Row, 1967. (Fiction)

Constant, Alberta. *Paintbrush on the Frontier: The Life and Times of George Caleb Bingham*. New York: Thomas Y. Crowell, 1974.

Cook, Olive Rambo. *Trails to Poosey*. Sebastopol, Calif.: Misty Hill Press, 1986.

Glubok, Shirley. *The Art of America from Jackson to Lincoln*. New York: Macmillan: 1973.

Hughes, Dean. *As Wide as the River*. Salt Lake City: Deseret, 1980. (Fiction)

————. *Under the Same Stars*. Salt Lake City: Deseret, 1979. (Fiction)

Wooldridge, Rhoda. *Hannah's Choice*. Independence, Mo.: Independence Press, 1984. (Fiction)

————. *Hannah's House*. Independence, Mo.: Independence Press, 1972. (Fiction)

————. *Hannah's Mill*. Independence, Mo.: Independence Press, 1984. (Fiction)

————. *That's the Way Joshuway*. Independence, Mo.: Independence Press, 1965. (Fiction)

Chapter 10

A DIVIDED COUNTRY

Find the answers to these questions as you read.

How were the North and South different?

What kind of life did a slave usually have?

Why did slaves sometimes run away?

Why was there a Civil War?

The American Civil War was one of the most terrible events in the history of the United States. In that war Americans fought each other. The people of the North fought the people of the South.

HOW THE NORTH AND THE SOUTH WERE DIFFERENT

Before the Civil War life in the Northern states was different from life in the Southern states. There were more people living in the Northern states than in the Southern states. The Northern states had more cities and more factories than the Southern states. There were many farms in both the Southern states and the North-

Slaves often worked in the fields from sunup to sundown.

State Historical Society of Missouri

ern states. Most Northern farmers lived on small farms. They grew many different crops. They raised mainly things to eat, such as corn, wheat, cattle, and hogs. Most Southerners were farmers. Many lived on small farms. But other Southerners lived on large farms called plantations. Cotton was the most important Southern crop. Some Southern farmers and plantation owners had slaves.

In some ways, it was good that the North and the South were not alike. They did not produce the same things. They could buy what they needed from each other. They could help each other. Sadly, the people of the South and the North did not always agree on what was best for the country.

The North wanted to place a special tax on things brought in from other countries. This tax was called a tariff. Most Southerners did not like the tariff. They believed that it mostly helped factory owners. There were not many factories in the South.

Northerners and Southerners disagreed most about slavery. You may remember reading in Chapter 5 that the Southern states allowed slavery, but the Northern states did not. Northerners did not want slavery in the North. Many of them also did not want African-Americans living in the North.

SLAVERY AND AFRICAN-AMERICANS

Most African-Americans lived in the Southern states before the Civil War. Most of them were slaves. They had not come to America by choice. They had been captured in Africa. They were brought to America in chains on crowded ships. When they got to America they were sold as slaves.

Slaves had very little freedom. They belonged to their owners, and so did their children. The slaves had to do whatever their

Slave cabins were small and plain.

Slaves were bought and sold at public sales.

State Historical Society of Missouri

Slaves sometimes ran away from their owners.

State Historical Society of Missouri

owners told them. When they did not, they were punished. Usually they received a whipping. Slaves could not own property. They could not have guns. They could not meet together unless a white person was there to watch them. In many states it was against the law to teach an African-American to read and write.

Slaves were treated like pieces of property, not like people. They were bought and sold. By the time of the Civil War a healthy slave sold for more than a thousand dollars.

Slaves had to work hard. They usually worked from sunup to sundown on every day except Sunday. Sunday was the one day when they could be with their families and have some fun. Slaves were not paid for their work. Their owners provided them with

When a slave family in Boone County ran away, their owner offered a $100 reward for their return.

State Historical Society of Missouri

$100 REWARD:

R AN AWAY from the subscriber, living in Boone county, Mo. on Friday the 13th June,

THREE NEGROES,

viz   DAVE, and JUDY his wife; and JOHN, their son. Dave is about 32 years of age, light color for a full blooded negro— is a good boot and shoe maker by trade : is also a good farm hand. He is about 5 feet 10 or 11 inches high, stout made, and quite an artful, sensible fellow. Had on when he went away, coat and pantaloons of brown woollen jeans, shirt of home made flax linen, and a pair of welted shoes. Judy is rather slender made, about 28 years old, has a very light complexion for a negro; had on a dress made of flax linen, striped with copperas and blue; is a first rate house servant and seamstress, and a good spinner, and is very full of affectation when spoken to. John is 9 years old, very likely and well grown; is remarkably light colored for a negro, and is cross-eyed. Had on a pair of brown jeans pantaloons, bleached flax linen shirt, and red flannel one under it, and a new straw hat.

I will give the above reward and all reasonable expenses, if secured any where out of the State, so that I can get them again, or $50 if taken within the State—$30 for Dave alone, and $20 for Judy and John, and the same in proportion out of the state. The above mentioned clothing was all they took with them from home, but it is supposed he had $30 or $40 in cash with him, so that he may buy and exchange their clothing.

WILLIAM LIENTZ.

Boone county, Mo. June 17, 1834:   52-2

food, clothes, and a place to live. Usually slaves lived in small cabins. Their food and their clothes were plain. Slaves did not live as well as their owners. Life was not very happy for slaves.

Some slaves asked the courts to set them free. Harriet and Dred Scott were Missouri slaves who became famous because they tried to win their freedom. They lost their case. The judges did not allow them to go free. But a St. Louis businessman later bought them and gave them their freedom.

Other slaves ran away. Most who did were caught and sent back to their masters. A few slaves did escape.

THE STORY OF A MISSOURI SLAVE

William Wells Brown was born in Kentucky. His mother was a slave. That meant that when he was born he was also a slave. When William was two years old, his master moved to Missouri. He took William and his other slaves with him. They lived on a farm at Marthasville. When he grew older, William had to work as a servant. William's mother had to work in the fields. William never knew his father.

William's master took him to St. Louis. He often had his slaves work for someone else. The owner kept the money his slaves earned from their jobs.

In St. Louis, William Brown worked in a hotel. The boss treated Brown and the other slaves that worked for him badly. He sometimes tied them up and whipped them. Brown tried to run away. He hid in the woods. The slave catchers came looking for him with a pack of dogs. He climbed a tree, but they found him. They put Brown in jail. Then they gave him a whipping for running away.

Brown's owner next arranged for him to work on a riverboat. When the steamboats were not running, Brown worked at the Missouri Hotel. He also worked in a printing office. The master sold Brown's mother and his brothers and sisters to different people in St. Louis. This broke up their family.

Brown thought about running away again, but he did not want

William Wells Brown was a slave who ran away from his owner. He became a doctor and a writer of books and plays.

State Historical Society of Missouri

to leave his mother. She was still a slave in St. Louis. Brown later had to work for a slave trader. He did not like it. He had to watch many cruel acts against other slaves.

Brown's owner decided to sell William. He wanted five hundred dollars for him. Brown found out that his sister had been sold to someone in another state. Before his sister left Missouri, Brown went to see her one last time. Her leaving made Brown and his mother very sad. They decided to try to run away. They crossed the Mississippi River and traveled for one hundred and fifty miles. A slave catcher found them. He brought them back to St. Louis and put them in jail.

They sent Brown's mother to New Orleans. The last time Brown saw his mother, she was chained to another woman on a steamboat going to New Orleans. Brown's owner sold him to another family. They took Brown with them to Ohio on a trip. Brown took advantage of being in a free state to make another attempt to

FAMOUS MISSOURIANS

John Berry Meachum

John Berry Meachum was a St. Louis pioneer. He became a teacher, a preacher, a businessman, and a leader. He did much to give African-Americans a better chance in life.

Meachum was born a slave in Virginia. He learned to be a carpenter, a cabinetmaker, and a cooper. A cooper was a person who made barrels. These were all important jobs. Persons with those skills could always find work.

Meachum was a slave. But he also was allowed to take extra jobs on the side. His owner let him keep some of the extra money he earned. Meachum used that money to buy freedom for himself and his father.

After he was free, Meachum moved to Kentucky. He married a slave. Her owner moved and took her to Missouri. Meachum followed them to Missouri.

Meachum arrived in St. Louis with only three dollars in his pocket. He did not have trouble finding a job. St. Louis was growing rapidly. There were not enough skilled workers there. Meachum saved his money. Before long he had enough money

run away. He walked off the boat at Cincinnati. Brown headed for Canada. This time he made it.

After he escaped, he worked on a steamer that ran on the Great Lakes between the United States and Canada. In that job

to buy freedom for his wife and their children.

Meachum built a steamboat. He ran it on the Mississippi River. People paid him to carry them and their goods. Soon he owned two brick houses in St. Louis and a farm in Illinois.

Meachum also became a Baptist minister. He started a church for African-Americans in St. Louis. It was the first black church in Missouri.

Meachum also began a school for black children in St. Louis. He wanted them to learn to read and write. At the time it was against the law to teach African-Americans to read and write. The officials closed his school.

He did not give up. Meachum built another steamboat. He used it as a school. The boat picked up the students and steamed out to the middle of the Mississippi River. The classes were held on the boat in the middle of the river. The officials in Missouri could not do anything about it. Meachum's school became known as the freedom school.

Meachum used much of the money that he made to buy slaves. He helped them go to school. Then he freed them. Meachum died before slavery was ended. But he worked to help blacks be free. All Missourians can be proud of this pioneer African-American leader.

he helped other runaway slaves to escape from their masters.

Brown was an abolitionist. An abolitionist was a person who was against slavery. He said that he only wanted black people to have an equal chance. Brown traveled to Europe. He studied medicine there. He was also an author. He wrote books and plays. He was one of the first American writers to tell about the importance of black people in history.

FREE BLACKS

Not all African-Americans were slaves. There were always a few free blacks. You will remember that Jeanette Fourchet was a free black woman in French Missouri. Free blacks did not have the same rights that white people had, but they were better off than slaves.

Free blacks worked as blacksmiths, gunsmiths, and cabinet-makers. Some ran businesses. Some were farmers, and others were teachers and ministers. A few free blacks became very successful. John Berry Meachum was a wealthy St. Louis black businessman. He owned a barrel factory and two steamboats. Hiram Young was a free black craftsman who ran the largest wagon factory in Independence.

TROUBLE ALONG THE MISSOURI-KANSAS BORDER

The slavery question divided the Northern and the Southern states. Southerners wanted to be able to take their slaves with them into the new lands in the West. Northerners did not want to allow slavery in those new lands. When settlers moved into Kansas, they began to fight over whether or not they should have slavery. Missourians became involved in the conflict in nearby Kansas.

Since Missouri was a slave state, most Missourians wanted Kansas to be a slave state. Missouri slaveholders were afraid that if Kansas became a free state their slaves would run away to Kansas, where they could be free. Missourians who wanted slavery sometimes crossed into Kansas carrying guns. They attacked the settlers in Kansas who did not want slavery. These Missourians were called Border Ruffians.

Some people from Kansas who did not want slavery made raids into Missouri. They were called Jayhawkers. They attacked Missourians who were for slavery. Many people were killed in the fighting over slavery in Kansas. Kansas was called Bleeding Kansas.

Not all Missourians wanted to let slavery into Kansas. Senator Thomas Hart Benton was against taking slaves into the West. Often he spoke against the spread of slavery. Many Missourians disagreed with him. He was defeated in an election because Missourians did not agree with him about the slavery question. The fighting in Kansas showed how serious the problem over slavery was.

CIVIL WAR COMES TO THE NATION

In 1860 Abraham Lincoln of Illinois was running for president of the United States. Lincoln thought that slavery was wrong. He did not want it to spread into the West. Most Northerners wanted Lincoln to be president.

Few Southerners voted for Lincoln. They did not like his ideas about slavery. Since the North had more voters, Lincoln won. Some Southern leaders believed that the North had taken over the national government. They were afraid that with Lincoln as president the United States government would favor the Northern states over the Southern states. Some even feared that the national government might try to get rid of slavery in the Southern states. There were already more free states than slave states.

Lincoln tried to calm their fears. The new president said that he would allow the states that already had slavery to keep it. But Lincoln's promises were not enough. Many Southerners believed that the national government was too powerful. They wanted the states to have more control. They were for states' rights.

Shortly after Lincoln was elected, South Carolina voted to leave the United States. It did not want to be a part of the United States any longer. Soon several other Southern states did the same thing. They formed another country and called it the Confederate

Abraham Lincoln is shown here with his son Tad.

Library of Congress

States of America. They elected Jefferson Davis of Mississippi to be their president.

President Lincoln did not think that states had the right to separate from the United States. He believed that it was his job as president to keep the country together. Southern leaders believed that they had the right to form a new country. The two sides were unable to settle their differences. Each was ready to fight to get what it wanted. The first shots were fired at Fort Sumter in South Carolina. The Civil War between the North and the South had begun. It was to be a long and terrible war.

New Words

cooper	cabinetmaker	property
Jayhawker	abolitionist	

Testing Yourself

1. In which part of the country were there more slaves?

2. Where were most of America's factories?

3. What was the most important crop in the South?

4. Which part of the country had the most people?

5. Who were some outstanding free blacks in Missouri?

6. Why was Kansas called Bleeding Kansas?

7. Why did the election of Abraham Lincoln cause some states to leave the Union?

 # Things to Talk About

1. Talk about the differences between living in the North and living in the South.

2. Write a list of the things wrong about slavery. Talk about these things in class.

3. Why do you think that William Wells Brown finally went to Canada?

 # True or False

Rewrite and correct each false statement on a separate sheet of paper.

1. Cotton was grown on plantations in the North.

2. Slaves were usually paid for their work.

3. Slaves sometimes ran away.

4. In many states it was against the law to teach an African-American to read and write.

5. Free blacks had the same rights as white people.

6. Abolitionists were for slavery.

7. People in the South voted for Abraham Lincoln for president.

Books You Can Read

Barry, James P. *Bloody Kansas, 1854–65: Guerrilla Warfare Delays Peaceful American Settlement.* New York: Franklin Watts, 1972.

Bell, Gertrude. *Posse of Two.* Eau Claire, Wisc.: Hale, 1964. (Fiction)

———. *Roundabout Road.* Independence, Mo.: Independence Press, 1972. (Fiction)

Hagler, Margaret. *Larry and the Freedom Man.* New York: Lathrop, 1959. (Fiction)

Spencer, Philip. *Three Against Slavery.* New York: Scholastic Book Services, 1974.

Chapter 11

THE CIVIL WAR COMES
TO MISSOURI

Find the answers to these questions as you read.

Why was the Civil War especially hard for Missourians?

What were some famous Civil War battles in Missouri?

What was guerrilla fighting?

How did women help fight the war?

Missouri was a border state. It was located between the North and the South. It was also a slave state. When the Civil War began, Missourians had to make a hard choice. They had to decide whether to support the North or the South. So did the people in many of the other slave states. Eleven slave states left the Union and joined the Confederate States of America. They were Texas, Arkansas, Louisiana, Mississippi, Alabama, Georgia, Florida, Tennessee, South Carolina, North Carolina, and Virginia. Not all of the slave states decided to become a part of the Confederacy. A few border states like Missouri did not break away from the United States of America.

FAMOUS MISSOURIANS

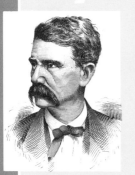

Francis P. Blair, Jr.

When the Civil War began, Missourians were divided. Some were for the North and the Union. Others were for the South and the Confederacy. As much as any other person, Francis P. Blair, Jr., helped keep Missouri in the Union.

Blair was born in Kentucky. His family called him Frank. His father had been a good friend of President Andrew Jackson. As a young boy Frank Blair met many famous American leaders. He decided that he wanted to become a politician. He went to Princeton University and studied law. Later he moved to St. Louis. He became a successful lawyer there.

Blair became more and more worried about the United States. He was afraid that the disagreements over slavery might split the country into two parts. Blair did not want this to happen.

Blair was a close friend of Abraham Lincoln. He was happy when Lincoln was elected president in 1860. He knew that Lincoln wanted to hold the country together.

When the Civil War began, Blair was worried.

A DIVIDED STATE

Some Missourians wanted to join the Southern states in their fight. Many Missouri slave owners were in this group. Missouri's governor was Claiborne Fox Jackson. He wanted Missouri to be-

But he worked hard to see that Missouri did not join the Confederacy. President Lincoln asked for troops from Missouri to fight for the Union. Blair quickly gathered and trained a group of men in St. Louis. They joined the Union Army. Many of Blair's soldiers were Germans. Blair worked with General Nathaniel Lyon, a Union officer who was killed during the Battle of Wilson's Creek.

During the war Blair fought in many battles. He was a good leader. He was promoted to the rank of general.

After the war Blair tried to end bitter feelings in his state. Many people wanted to punish anyone who had worked for the South. Frank Blair believed that this was wrong. Many of his old friends did not like this, but many others agreed with Blair.

During his career Blair held many important offices. He was a United States senator. He also served in the United States House of Representatives. After the war he ran for the office of vice-president of the United States. Blair lost the election. But it was an honor to have been chosen to run for that important office. A statue of Blair stands in Statuary Hall in the United States Capitol Building. He is one of two Missourians chosen for this honor. The other Missourian selected is Senator Thomas Hart Benton.

come a part of the Confederate States of America.

Other Missourians wanted their state to remain in the United States. Many of Missouri's German people joined this group. Francis P. Blair, Jr., worked hard to keep Missouri in the Union.

The Confederate and Union groups fought to run the state.

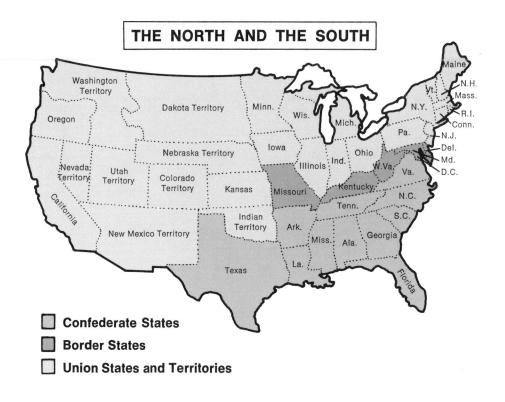

THE NORTH AND THE SOUTH

Washington Territory
Oregon
Dakota Territory
Minn.
Wis.
Mich.
Maine
N.H.
Mass.
Vt.
N.Y.
R.I.
Conn.
Pa.
N.J.
Nevada Territory
Utah Territory
Colorado Territory
Nebraska Territory
Iowa
Ohio
Del.
Md.
D.C.
Kansas
Missouri
Illinois
Ind.
W.Va.
Va.
California
Indian Territory
Ark.
Kentucky
Tenn.
N.C.
S.C.
New Mexico Territory
Miss.
Ala.
Georgia
Texas
La.
Florida

☐ **Confederate States**
■ **Border States**
☐ **Union States and Territories**

Union soldiers went to Jefferson City. Governor Jackson was forced to leave the capital city because he supported the South. The people who wanted to keep Missouri in the Union won. They chose a new governor to replace Governor Jackson. Jackson kept on fighting for the South. So did some other Missourians.

Even though Missouri did not leave the Union, its men served in both the Union and the Confederate armies. Many Missourians fought for the North. Some African-Americans became Union soldiers. Union soldiers wore blue uniforms. Other Missourians fought for the South. Confederate soldiers wore gray uniforms. Some Missourians chose not to fight for either side. They wanted to stay out of the war.

Since Missouri was a divided state, it had some special problems. Neighbors fought one another. Sometimes one brother in a family would fight for the North, and another brother would fight for the South. The war tore these families apart. Many Missourians were injured or killed in the fighting. The death of so many people brought sadness into many Missouri homes during the Civil War.

THE WAR IN MISSOURI

Missouri became a battleground during the Civil War. The North controlled Missouri during the war. Most of the larger battles in Missouri happened when Confederate fighters tried to take Missouri away from the North.

General Sterling Price was a famous Missouri leader who fought for the South. Before the Civil War he had been governor of Missouri. He and Claiborne Jackson formed an army made up of

General Sterling Price was an important Confederate military leader.

State Historical Society of Missouri

Missourians who wanted to fight for the South. They also got some help from Confederate soldiers from other states.

THE BATTLES OF WILSON'S CREEK AND LEXINGTON

Sterling Price's troops fought in one of the most important early battles in the Civil War. This battle took place at Wilson's Creek near Springfield. General Nathaniel Lyon was the leader of the Union army at Wilson's Creek. The fighting was very hard.

One out of every six men in the battle was either killed or hurt. General Lyon died at Wilson's Creek. Price and his men forced the Union army to retreat. But Price's troops were not strong enough to defeat the Northern forces completely at Wilson's Creek. The battlefield at Wilson's Creek is a historic site. Many visitors go there every year.

The Battle of Wilson's Creek was an early Civil War battle fought near Springfield.

State Historical Society of Missouri

Southern soldiers hid behind hemp bales to protect themselves from gunfire during the Battle of Lexington.

After the Battle of Wilson's Creek, Price marched his men north. He wanted to take all of Missouri. He was also looking for more men to fight for the South. Price reached the town of Lexington on the Missouri River. There were Union troops in Lexington.

Lexington was built on a hill. To take the hill, Price's men needed to protect themselves from the gunfire. They soaked hemp bales in the Missouri River. Hemp was a Missouri crop used for making rope. They rolled the wet bales ahead of them as they climbed the hill. The bales stopped the lead bullets from hitting the soldiers. Price and his men captured Lexington. But they soon had to retreat into Arkansas. Price did not have enough soldiers to defend the town if the Union sent more troops there.

Today in Lexington you can still see the battlefield and Anderson House. Anderson House was used as a hospital during the

The Lafayette County Courthouse in Lexington was hit by a cannonball during a Civil War battle.

Missouri Division of Tourism

battle. A cannonball has been put on the front of the Lafayette County courthouse where one landed during the battle. Sometimes groups of people dressed as Confederate and Union soldiers reenact the battle of Lexington.

OTHER MISSOURI CIVIL WAR BATTLES

Later in the war, General Price came back to Missouri. He tried again to take Missouri for the Confederates. He entered Missouri from the southeast and marched north with his army. He wanted to take St. Louis. First, he hoped to capture Fort Davidson. Fort Davidson was a Union fort at Pilot Knob, south of St. Louis. Price was not able to take Fort Davidson. He then decided to march his soldiers toward Jefferson City. His troops fought small battles at Jefferson City, Boonville, and Lexington.

Then Price headed for Kansas City. He had a large army when

he neared the city. But a stronger Union army was waiting for him. The Battle of Westport lasted three days. Finally Price's men became too worn out to fight any more. His Southern troops left Missouri for good.

GUERRILLA FIGHTING

Not all of the fighting in Missouri was done by soldiers in the Union and Confederate armies. Bands of armed men called guerrillas also fought in Missouri. They were also known as bushwhackers because they hid in the bushes and the woods. They would attack and then run away. The Confederate guerrillas wanted the South to win. They hated the Union soldiers who had come into Missouri.

Bill Anderson was a Confederate guerrilla leader who killed many people. His nickname was "Bloody Bill."

State Historical Society of Missouri

The Southern guerrillas attacked the Union troops. They destroyed railroads and bridges. They also attacked Missouri families who supported the North. The Northern guerrillas attacked people who wanted the South to win the war. The guerrillas on both sides were very cruel. They killed many people. Some guerrillas and bushwhackers were outlaws who used the war as an excuse to kill and rob. William C. Quantrill, "Bloody" Bill Anderson, Cole Younger, Jesse James, and Frank James were Missouri guerrillas.

The Union soldiers hated and feared the Southern guerrillas. Sometimes the Union troops in Missouri behaved like the guerrillas. They killed and mistreated people whom they believed were helping the Confederate guerrillas. The Union army also forced people in western Missouri to leave their homes. The guerrilla fighting in Missouri created much suffering on both sides.

MISSOURI WOMEN AND THE CIVIL WAR

Women also did their part. They had to take care of family farms and businesses while their husbands and sons were away fighting. They worked in their homes preparing food and clothing for wounded soldiers. They also rolled bandages. A few volunteered to serve as nurses on the battlefield. They helped start the Western Sanitary Commission in St. Louis. It was an organization that did the same kinds of things that the Red Cross did in later wars. Women also raised money to help take care of people who had been forced to leave their homes because of the fighting.

Mary Whitney Phelps was a Springfield woman who showed great courage during the Civil War. She visited the battlefields at Wilson's Creek and at Pea Ridge (just over the Missouri border in Arkansas). She helped take care of the wounded soldiers.

After the war, Phelps was concerned about the children left with no parents. She started an orphanage in Springfield. Children of both Union and Confederate soldiers could live there. Phelps's work became well known. The United States Congress gave her twenty thousand dollars to run the orphanage.

Women sometimes nursed wounded soldiers on the battlefield during the Civil War.

HOW THE WAR AFFECTED ONE MISSOURI FAMILY

Willard and Mollie Mendenhall were a young married couple living on a farm near Lexington, Missouri, when the Civil War began. They had two children at the time. Willard and Mollie worked on their farm. He also owned a business in Lexington that built carriages.

When General Sterling Price and his Confederate troops fought with the Union forces at Lexington, a part of the battle took place very close to the Mendenhalls' house. The Mendenhalls watched the bloody battle. Price defeated the Yankee soldiers in the battle. That made the Mendenhalls happy. They wanted the South to win the war, but Willard decided to stay in Lexington. He did not join the Confederate army.

The Union soldiers returned to Lexington after General Price took his troops to Arkansas. The Northern soldiers did not trust the Mendenhalls because they were for the South. They searched their house for guns. Mollie hid a pistol belonging to the family under her dress. The soldiers took over the building Mendenhall used for his carriage factory. They used it for their supplies.

One Sunday when the Mendenhalls went to Lexington to go to church, they found that the Union soldiers had closed six of the town's eight churches. The Union leaders thought that some of the people in those churches supported the South.

In the diary he kept, Mendenhall reported that soldiers and bushwhackers from both sides often burned houses. They also took food, crops, and supplies from the people living around Lexington. The Union forces took a pair of mules and some crops belonging to the Mendenhalls. The war ruined the Mendenhalls' carriage-making business. They had to borrow money to pay some of their bills. Fortunately, none of the Mendenhalls were hurt. Many of their neighbors were not so lucky. The bushwhackers shot and killed several people living in the area. The Civil War years were hard times for the Mendenhalls and for many Missourians.

THE WAR ENDS

The Civil War lasted four years. The Confederate armies surrendered in 1865. They agreed to stop fighting. More than six hundred thousand Americans died in the war.

More people died as a result of disease than died in battle. During the Civil War, doctors did not have the medicines we have today. They had no way to fight infections. Even a minor wound could cause a person to die.

The war brought the Confederate states back into the Union. It also ended slavery in the United States.

 **New Words**

retreat	bale	control
uniform	border	troops
cannonball	infection	officer
rank	diary	guerrilla

 Testing Yourself

1. What famous Missouri leader worked hard to keep the state in the Union?
2. Did the Union keep control of Missouri's government during the Civil War?
3. How did General Price's soldiers help to keep themselves from getting hurt in the Battle of Lexington?
4. How did guerrillas fight?
5. What were two results of the Civil War?

 Things to Do

1. Pretend that you were living in Missouri during the Civil War. Write a letter to a friend telling what life was like in Missouri during the war.
2. On a map of the United States color the Union states blue. Color the border states brown. Color the Confederate states red. Do not color those states that had not yet been formed.

Fill in the Blanks

On a separate sheet of paper, rewrite the following sentences. Fill each blank with the proper word.

1. ═══════ ═══════ was president of the United States during the Civil War.

2. The Southern states formed a new country which they called the ═══════ ═══════ ═══════ ═══════.

3. Another name for the United States was the ═══════.

4. The Northern soldiers wore ═══════ uniforms.

5. The Southern soldiers wore ═══════ uniforms.

6. Most Germans in Missouri wanted the ═══════ to win the Civil War.

7. Because it was located between the North and the South, Missouri was a ═══════ state.

8. The ═══════ won the Civil War.

 Things to Talk About

1. Do you think Abraham Lincoln might have owned slaves? Why or why not?

2. Why do you think black Missourians chose to fight for the Union?

3. How did Jesse and Frank James get started as outlaws?

4. Were any Civil War battles fought near your community? If so, try to find out something about them. Someone from a historical society in your area may be able to tell you what happened during the Civil War in your part of the state.

5. Why is a Civil War the worst kind of a war?

 ## Books You Can Read

Archer, Myrtle. *The Young Boys Gone*. New York: Walker, 1978. (Fiction)

Baldwin, Margaret, and Pat O'Brien. *Wanted: Frank and Jesse James: The Real Story*. New York: Julian Messner, 1981.

Bell, Gertrude. *First Crop*. Independence, Mo.: Independence Press, 1973. (Fiction)

———. *Where Runs the River*. Independence, Mo.: Independence Press, 1976. (Fiction)

Colby, C. B. *Civil War Weapons*. New York: Coward, McCann and Geoghegan, 1962.

Dick, Trella Lamson. *The Island on the Border: A Civil War Story*. New York: Abelard-Schuman, 1963. (Fiction)

Erdman, Loula Grace. *Another Spring*. New York: Dodd, Mead, and Co., 1966. (Fiction)

Katz, William. *An Album of the Civil War*. New York: Franklin Watts, 1974.

Levenson, Dorothy. *The First Book of the Civil War*. New York: Franklin Watts, 1968.

Chapter 12

RECONSTRUCTION IN MISSOURI

Find the answers to these questions as you read.

What was Reconstruction?

Who were the Radicals?

What was life like for African-Americans after the Civil War?

The time after the Civil War is called Reconstruction. The word *reconstruction* means to build again. There was much to be done in Missouri.

In Missouri the guerrilla raids and the Civil War battles had destroyed many homes, farms, buildings, railroads, and bridges. The damage in Missouri was worse than in most Northern states. But Missouri was not as badly damaged as many Southern states. Missourians worked hard to rebuild their state after the war. Before long, Missouri farmers were raising more crops than before the war. More people were coming to live in the state. Missourians reopened stores, factories, and businesses that had been closed during the war. They also started new ones. Missourians also built new railroads. The state was growing again.

HEALING OLD WOUNDS

It was hard to fix buildings and repair bridges. It was even harder to end the bad feelings. Men and women who supported the South believed they had been right. Union supporters thought they had been right. It was hard for them to understand each other. It was harder for them to forgive each other.

There was still another problem. How should the government treat people who had helped the South? Some people, called Radicals, felt these people should be punished. Other people believed that the Southern supporters had already suffered enough.

PRESIDENT LINCOLN IS SHOT

Abraham Lincoln knew how much both the North and South had suffered during the war. He wanted peace. He felt it was time to end the angry feelings. He did not want to punish the South or its people. The Radicals disagreed with Lincoln. They did not want to let Confederate supporters vote or run for office.

Just as the war was ending, President and Mrs. Lincoln went to Ford's Theater in Washington, D.C., to see a play. John Wilkes Booth was an actor who had wanted the South to win the war. He shot and killed President Lincoln while he and Mrs. Lincoln were watching the play. Lincoln's death was a big loss for the country.

Vice-President Andrew Johnson became president. The Radicals in Congress did not like President Johnson. They became more powerful. They passed laws that took away some Southern rights. These laws kept Southern supporters from voting and holding office.

After the Civil War it did not take long for business to improve in Missouri. This is a drawing of the crowded wharfs at St. Louis in 1871.

State Historical Society of Missouri

RADICALS IN MISSOURI

Radical leaders in Missouri were in charge of the state at the end of the war. They passed some harsh laws. People who had helped the South could not vote in Missouri. They could not hold public office. They could not work as lawyers, teachers, or ministers in the state.

Other Missourians wanted to restore good feelings between the two sides as soon as possible. People like Frank Blair worked to get rid of the harsh Radical laws. Before long those laws were changed. Missouri voters chose Francis Marion Cockrell to be a United States senator from Missouri. He had been a general in the Confederate army.

The Radicals did some good things for the state. They had helped end slavery in Missouri. The Radicals rebuilt schools destroyed during the war and started new ones. They opened schools for blacks. They also established schools to train teachers. The Radicals worked to build new railroads and to make business grow in the state.

AFRICAN-AMERICANS AFTER THE WAR

After the Civil War, all blacks were free citizens, but they still did not have equal rights with whites. Blacks wanted to earn a good living and enjoy a better life. They wanted to be able to hold the same kinds of jobs as white people. Those changes were not easy to get. Even many Missouri leaders who had been against slavery did not favor giving African-Americans equal rights.

African-Americans of all ages wanted to go to school after the Civil War.

State Historical Society of Missouri

James Milton Turner

The Civil War ended slavery in the United States. But African-Americans still could not vote in Missouri. Just after the war there were no public schools for blacks in the state.

James Milton Turner believed that this was wrong. He knew what it was like to be a black person in Missouri. He wanted to change things. He believed that in America all people should be treated equally.

Not all Missourians agreed with Turner. Once an angry mob tried to get Turner. They stood around the house where he was staying. To escape, Turner ran from the house barefoot through the snow. He faced problems all his life.

Turner was born a slave in St. Louis County. His parents were slaves. His father, John, was a very good animal doctor. People came to John Turner for help in caring for their sick animals. John Turner's owner let him keep some of the money they paid him. He used that money to buy his own freedom. But John Turner's wife and children were still slaves. He worked hard to earn enough money to buy freedom for them.

When James Milton was four years old, his father bought him for fifty dollars. As James Milton became older, his parents wanted him to go to school. That was not easy. A Missouri law said that black children could not be taught to read and write.

James Milton went to John Berry Meachum's school in St. Louis. But officials closed Meachum's school. Meachum then started a school on a steamboat in the Mississippi River. James Milton Turner went to that school.

Turner worked as an office boy in St. Louis. He decided he wanted more education. He heard about Oberlin College in Ohio. Oberlin was very different from most other colleges at that time. It was the first college that allowed both men and women to attend. It was also open to both black students and white students. Turner went to school there for a time. But he had to return to St. Louis.

The Civil War came. Turner became a servant for a Union Army officer. He was at the Battle of Wilson's Creek. Later he was wounded in the hip during the Battle of Shiloh. His wound made him limp for the rest of his life. He returned to St. Louis. During the rest of the war, Turner helped runaway slaves escape into Illinois.

After the Civil War, Turner worked to get equal treatment for blacks. He became a leader of the Missouri Equal Rights League. The league was a group of both white and black persons. They believed African-Americans should be able to vote and have good schools.

Turner also helped raise money for Lincoln Institute in Jefferson City. This school was for African-Americans. Today it is called Lincoln University.

Turner became a teacher. He taught in Missouri's first public school for blacks. It was in Kansas City. Turner then went to Boonville. There he ran the black schools for the city. Later the governor of Missouri asked him to help start public schools for African-American children in all parts of the state.

Turner also became one of America's first African-American diplomats. President Ulysses S. Grant named him to represent the United States government in the African country of Liberia. Turner later returned to St. Louis. For a short time he ran a factory in St. Louis that made farm tools.

Turner had studied law on his own. He worked as a lawyer for some black slaves who had once been owned by Cherokee Indians in Oklahoma. He tried to protect their rights.

James Milton Turner had many disappointments in his life. He did not live long enough to see African-Americans get the rights he wanted them to have. But he had been one of Missouri's first civil rights leaders.

Black soldiers from Missouri gave money to establish Lincoln University in Jefferson City.

James Milton Turner was a former slave who became a leader in Missouri during Reconstruction. He worked for a law giving African-Americans the right to vote in Missouri. He also worked to establish schools for blacks. Most African-Americans had not learned to read and write. In Missouri it had been against the law for a black person to go to school. After the war Missouri opened its first public schools for black children. African-Americans also raised money to help get schools started. Black soldiers from Missouri gave money to establish Lincoln University in Jefferson City. They wanted a college to train black teachers.

Other groups helped start schools for black Missourians. The American Missionary Association sent Mrs. C. A. Briggs to Warrensburg to teach classes for former slaves. Mrs. Briggs was a white schoolteacher from Minnesota. Her husband had been killed while fighting in the Civil War. She wanted to start a school for blacks. She had to raise money to buy books and supplies for her students. She also had to teach classes in the evenings. Most of her pupils had to work during the day. After working all day they were tired. But they still came to school at night. They wanted to get an education.

Black churches were very important. African-Americans organized and ran their own churches. Black ministers often became leaders in African-American communities.

Blacks won a few victories in politics. African-Americans had gained the right to vote and to hold office. Blanche K. Bruce and Hiram Revels became the first two blacks to serve in the United State Senate. They were elected in Mississippi. But both men had lived in Missouri at one time. Revels once ran a school for black children in St. Louis.

Still, blacks were not allowed to do everything whites could. Missouri was a segregated state. Life was hard for black people in Missouri after the war. But some former slaves became very successful.

Bettie and Charles Birthright were former slaves who became very successful after the Civil War.

Dunklin County Museum

FORMER SLAVES BUILD A NEW LIFE IN MISSOURI

Bettie and Charles Birthright had both been slaves. The ending of slavery made them free persons. After the Civil War they decided to live in Clarkton, Missouri. Charles worked as a barber. Bettie earned money by sewing and baking. She made fancy clothes, and she also baked fine cakes. They saved their money. They used it to buy land. Soon they were also running a large farm. They owned over five hundred acres of land. They rented some of their land to cotton farmers. They also made loans to people in Clarkton.

The Birthrights were members of the Presbyterian Church in Clarkton. Charles was a good musician. He played the violin and led the town's orchestra. When the people of Clarkton decided to build a school, Charles gave more money than anyone else in town. When the Birthrights died, they donated a large amount of their money to a school in Alabama that educated black ministers.

Women tried to get the right to vote after the Civil War.

State Historical Society of Missouri

WOMEN SEEK THE RIGHT TO VOTE

Women also worked to get equal treatment after the Civil War. They especially wanted the right to vote and to run for public office. Virginia Minor was an early leader in the movement in Missouri to give women the right to vote. In 1869 there was a national meeting held in St. Louis to support voting for women. Women did not get the vote in Missouri until 1920.

 # New Words

Reconstruction	rights	segregated
damage	lawyer	limp
harsh	hatred	diplomat
equal		

 # Testing Yourself

1. What were some of the problems Missourians faced after the Civil War?

2. What happened to Abraham Lincoln just as the war was ending?

3. What good things happened during Radical rule in Missouri?

4. What Missouri leader worked hard to do away with Radical laws punishing the Confederates?

5. What did African-Americans do to improve their lives after the Civil War?

6. What two groups worked to get the right to vote in Missouri after the Civil War?

Choose the Right Words

Select the right words to complete each of these sentences. Then rewrite each sentence correctly on another sheet of paper.

1. The war damage in Missouri was (less, more) than in many of the Southern states.

2. During Reconstruction many people (came to, left) the state.

3. Missourians elected Frances Marion Cockrell to be a United States Senator in 1875. He had been a (Union, Confederate) general.

4. Hiram R. Revels became one of the first black (United States senators, Missouri governors).

Books You Can Read

Cook, Olive Rambo. *Locket.* New York: David McKay, 1963. (Fiction)

————. *Serilda's Star.* New York: Longmans, 1959. (Fiction)

Ernst, John. *Jesse James.* Englewood Cliffs, N.J.: Prentice-Hall, 1976.

Levenson, Dorothy. *A First Book of Reconstruction.* New York: Franklin Watts, 1970.

Chapter 13

CHANGING TIMES IN MISSOURI

Find the answers to these questions as you read.

What new inventions were changing the way people in Missouri lived?

How did people light their homes before the invention of electric lights?

What was the Louisiana Purchase Exposition?

What was the difference between a general store and a department store?

The years just after the Civil War brought many changes to the United States and to Missouri. New inventions made life easier for many Americans.

Thomas Edison invented the electric light bulb. Before his invention, people lighted their homes and businesses with kerosene lamps or candles. In the cities there were also some gas lights. Inventions like Edison's light bulb increased the demand for electricity. Before 1900 only a few people in the cities had electricity.

Another important invention was the telephone. Alexander Graham Bell invented it. At first people thought of the telephone as just a toy. But when they saw how useful the telephone was, many Americans wanted one.

There were many other popular new inventions. Thomas Edison's phonograph brought musical recordings into homes. George Eastman's box camera let ordinary people take photographs. The electric vacuum cleaner and the electric iron made household chores easier. Indoor toilets, bathtubs, and hot and cold running water were important new additions in some American homes. The first automobiles were also built at this time. They were called "horseless carriages."

THE LOUISIANA PURCHASE EXPOSITION

Many of these new inventions were displayed at the Louisiana Purchase Exposition in St. Louis in 1904. It was a great fair held to celebrate the one hundredth birthday of the Louisiana Purchase. Most people called it the St. Louis World's Fair. The fair was supposed to begin in 1903. It was not ready to open until 1904.

The people of St. Louis built hundreds of buildings in Forest Park just for the fair. They invited people from all over the world to come to the fair. Sixty-two foreign nations set up displays telling about their countries. Every state except Delaware had a building to show things at the fair.

The fairgrounds covered over twelve hundred acres. At night thousands of electric bulbs lighted the fairgrounds. They were a thrilling sight. More than twenty million people visited the fair. Most were not disappointed with what they saw.

A ST. LOUIS BOY AT THE WORLD'S FAIR

Edward Coff was a twelve-year-old boy who lived in St. Louis in 1904. This was a very exciting time to be in St. Louis. Edward had watched the workers put up the buildings on the fairgrounds for the World's Fair. His father owned furniture stores in St. Louis. He had

Many new buildings were built in Forest Park for the Louisiana Purchase Exposition.

to open new stores to handle the extra business from people getting ready for the fair. People all over the city needed more furniture. They were planning to rent out their spare rooms to the visitors who came to see the fair.

Edward visited the fair at least twelve times during the summer of 1904. His favorite place at the fair was the Pike. The Pike was a long street lined on both sides with amusement rides and exhibits. There was a fun house with slides, turning barrels, and funny mirrors. There was also a ride called "Under and Over the Sea." It was a submarine that went into a big tank of water.

The "Wild West Show" at the fair had Indian people dressed in their tribal costumes. At another show, a man mounted on a horse dived from a high cliff into a pool of water. There was a wild animal show. There were also many restaurants and concession stands. A St. Louis waffle maker made some of the first ice-cream cones in America and sold them at the fair.

Each time Edward went to the fair his mother gave him a dollar.

The Pike was a long street at the World's Fair in St. Louis. There were amusement rides and exhibits along both sides.

It did not take him long to spend it. He always ran out of money before he got to the giant Ferris Wheel. It cost twenty-five cents to ride the Ferris Wheel. It was 260 feet high. It had thirty-six cars. Each of the cars held sixty people. People at the fair could also take a ride in a great hot-air balloon.

When he had spent his money, Edward visited the free exhibits. In one building there were tanks of water holding all kinds of fish. Edward liked to watch the sea horses. He also visited the Japanese garden and the Swiss Mountain village. At one village from another land, Edward watched the people making a stew with vegetables and dog meat. He also watched the birds in the giant Bird Cage. That cage is still used today at the St. Louis Zoo in Forest Park.

There were many other exhibits. The Palace of Electricity was filled with new electrical inventions. There were waterfalls and fountains pouring water into a great lagoon. Like most visitors to the fair, Edward never ran out of things to see. It is not surprising that so many people went to the fair.

One of the most popular songs in America in 1904 was "Meet Me in Saint Louie." People everywhere were singing:

> Meet me in Saint Louie, Louie,
> Meet me at the Fair,
> Don't tell me the lights are shining,
> Any place but there.
> We'll dance the hootchie-kootchie,
> I'll be your tootsie-wootsie,
> If you'll meet me in Saint Louie, Louie,
> Meet me at the Fair.

Some people traveled to the fair in horse-drawn carriages. A few even drove there in one of the new "horseless carriages." But most of the visitors came to St. Louis by train.

RAILROADS IN MISSOURI

In 1904 a person could travel to most parts of Missouri by train. Railroads had become the best way to travel and to transport goods. They had replaced steamboats as the most important form of transportation in the state. The railroads helped cities like St. Louis, Kansas City, St. Joseph, Sedalia, Springfield, and Joplin grow.

In the Ozarks, the railroads helped the lumber industry. Sawmills were set up in many Ozark counties. Many new people came to the Ozarks to cut timber and to work in the sawmills. Railroads used wooden ties to hold their rails in place. Builders needed lumber for new buildings. The railroads provided a way to transport Missouri wood products to where they were needed.

The railroads also helped the mining industry in Missouri grow. Lead, zinc, and coal were the state's top three mineral products

Railroads helped the lumber industry in the Ozarks. This picture shows a log train arriving at a sawmill in Winona.

State Historical Society of Missouri

after the Civil War.

Railroad construction was expensive. Crossing rivers caused railroad builders a problem. After the Civil War engineers developed new and better ways to build bridges across the state's biggest rivers. The Burlington Railroad built a bridge across the Missouri River at Kansas City. It was called the Hannibal Bridge. Four thousand trains used it to cross the Missouri River during the first eight months after it was built. Kansas City became an important railroad center.

Building a bridge across the Mississippi River at St. Louis was an even more difficult job. The river was very wide and deep at St. Louis. Many engineers did not believe that a bridge could be built there. James B. Eads proved that they were wrong. He designed the Eads Bridge. He used steel to make his bridge strong. He also used a diving bell so that the men could work underwater. Bridge building was dangerous work. Several men lost their lives while

The Eads Bridge was built across the Mississippi River at St. Louis. It is still considered one of the world's great bridges.

Charles Treft photograph; courtesy State Historical Society of Missouri

working on the Eads Bridge.

Many people were amazed when the beautiful Eads Bridge was finished. Even today it is considered to be one of the world's great bridges.

AUTOMOBILES COME TO MISSOURI

Missourians began to drive automobiles about 1890. These first "horseless carriages" were very different from the cars of today. At first only wealthy people could afford automobiles. Many Missourians did not like them. They believed that they were dangerous. Automobiles often frightened horses they met on the road.

The early automobiles could not go very fast. But the state government did not want to take any chances with speeders. The

Horses pull a car out of the mud in Jefferson County.

State Historical Society of Missouri

Bicycle riding was popular in Missouri. These riders were from St. Louis.

State Historical Society of Missouri

Missouri General Assembly passed a law setting the speed limit at nine miles an hour.

The first automobiles had another problem. They had to travel mostly on narrow, dirt roads made for wagons. Cars often got stuck in mud. Car owners sometimes had to get someone with a team of horses to pull their car out of the mud. As more people got cars, Missouri had to take steps to build better roads.

BICYCLES

Many Missourians began riding bicycles for fun. The first bicycles had high front wheels. But the newer ones with both wheels the same size were easier and safer to ride. Bicycle riding became a popular activity for both women and men. Sometimes they rode together on a bicycle built for two.

TELEPHONES COME TO MISSOURI

Missouri got its first telephones after the Civil War. Wires had to be strung from house to house in each town. This took time.

St. Louis, Hannibal, and Kansas City all had early telephone systems. Missouri's first callers could not talk long-distance. It took a long time to string telephone wires across the state. Even then, only people in Kansas City and St. Louis could call each other. In the years that followed, many miles of telephone wires were stretched across the country.

FACTORIES AND THE GROWTH OF CITIES

Before the Civil War there were only a few factories in the state. Most shoes, tools, and clothing were made in small shops. Often only one or two people worked in these shops. They used mostly simple hand tools.

FAMOUS MISSOURIANS

Susan Elizabeth Blow

People in St. Louis have often tried new ideas to make city life better. St. Louis was the first American city to have kindergartens in the public schools

The first kindergartens were in Germany. Susan Blow and her family were traveling in Europe, an she visited several kindergartens there.

After she returned home, she decided to start a kindergarten in St. Louis. She talked to William Torrey Harris, the superintendent of the St. Louis schools. He encouraged her. She went to New Yor to learn more about kindergartens. Susan Blow came back to Missouri and opened a small kinder garten in her home.

The next year Harris gave her a room at the Des Peres School in St. Louis. Blow agreed to teach without pay. The school hired one person to help

Missouri Capitol mural by Gari Melchers; courtesy State Historical Society of Missouri

More people were moving to Missouri. They needed more products than the small workshops could provide. Small shops grew into factories. Most of the new factories were built in cities. The factories used new and expensive machinery to make the products. The new factories needed more workers. People moved from farms and small towns into the larger cities to work in the factories. Each year the number of factory workers grew.

Workers had moved to the cities to find better jobs. But they were often disappointed. Some factory owners paid their workers very little. Both grown-ups and children had to work to earn enough money to pay the bills. It was not unusual for young

her. She also had two unpaid helpers. Thirty-eight children were in Blow's first public kindergarten.

Blow believed that kindergartens should be happy places where children would want to learn. She used plants and other decorations to make her classroom cheerful. The children learned about colors, shapes, and numbers by using colored blocks and balls. They also learned by singing songs.

Many people liked Blow's ideas. Within three years the St. Louis schools had thirty kindergartens. No other city in the United States had as many public kindergartens.

Who would teach all these new kindergartens? Blow wanted to make sure there would be enough good teachers. She opened a school to teach teachers how to run kindergartens.

Susan Blow's kindergartens in St. Louis were copied by other cities in America. Susan Blow was an outstanding leader. She helped children all over America get a better start in school.

children to work all day in the factories. Some factories were dangerous places to work.

Workers sometimes formed labor unions. They hoped to get more money for their work. They also wanted safer factories. Sometimes the workers refused to work. This was called a strike. Unions used strikes to try to get higher wages and better working conditions.

St. Louis had more factories than any other Missouri city. Shoes, medicines, beer, chewing tobacco, clothes, machines, iron ware, and food products were all made in St. Louis.

Kansas City also began to grow after the Civil War. Many peo-

The Kansas City Stockyards helped Kansas City grow after the Civil War.

ple had left the city during the war because of the fighting there. After the war, they moved back to Kansas City to work in the new factories.

The meat-packing plants were important in Kansas City. Western ranchers sent their cattle to the Kansas City Stockyards on railroad cars. The meat-packers killed the animals. They made the beef into canned meat. The canned meat would not spoil, and it could be shipped to eastern cities very easily. Later, the meat-packers began shipping fresh meat in refrigerator cars.

Another kind of factory in Kansas City was the flour-milling plant. After the war, farmers in Kansas and Missouri began to grow more wheat. Grain dealers built mills to grind the wheat into flour.

St. Joseph was another Missouri city that grew because of meat-packing. New factories at Springfield made furniture, flour, lumber, cotton and wool cloth, and wagons. Springfield became an important city in the southern part of the state. So did Joplin. Mining was the most important activity there.

FARMING

Farming has always been important in Missouri. You have already read about the life of the pioneer farmer. After the Civil War, many new farms were started in Missouri.

Farmers began using even more machines. Corn planters, binders, threshing machines, hay balers, corn shellers, and plows with wheels and a seat for the driver could now be found on many Missouri farms. Horses or mules still pulled most of these new machines. A few were run by steam engines.

Missouri farmers began to look for new ways to grow better crops. They used new fertilizers and better kinds of seeds. The University of Missouri School of Agriculture was started in 1870. Scientists there helped find better ways to farm.

Missouri's most important crops were corn, wheat, barley, tobacco, hay, fruit, and vegetables. Farmers also raised cattle, hogs, horses, mules, sheep, and chickens.

Missouri became famous for its horses. An important horse show and sale was held every year in Mexico, Missouri. People came to it from all over the country.

Tom Bass was a Missourian who became a famous horse trainer. He was known throughout the world. Bass had been born a slave. He trained many well-known horses. One of the horses he trained was chosen the best saddle horse in the United States. The horse's name was Rex McDonald.

Leaders in Kansas City organized the American Royal Horse and Livestock Show. It remains one of the largest such shows in the United States today.

MISSOURI STORES

As Missouri grew and changed, its people bought more of their things from stores. The new factories produced goods more cheaply. The railroads moved them from the factories to the stores. Families no longer had to make most of the things they needed. They were now consumers. They used goods that other

Many Missouri towns had a general store. This one was at Creve Coeur.

State Historical Society of Missouri

people made for them. Shopping became an important activity.

People living on farms and in small towns shopped in general stores. A general store was usually a one-room building. Its walls were lined with shelves.

The food was on one side of the store. Tea, coffee, beans, peas, rice, and cornmeal were kept in bins behind the counter. Smaller metal cans held salt, pepper, cinnamon, cloves, and nutmeg. Wooden kegs contained butter, pickles, and chewing tobacco. These were usually kept in front of the grocery counter. There were also barrels of vinegar, kerosene, and molasses. The customers would tell a clerk what they wanted. Then the clerk would carefully measure the exact amount from the large container.

The most popular part of the general store for children was the glass candy counter. In it were many kinds of candy. Two favorite kinds were stick candy and licorice.

In another part of the store, tools were sold. One could find nails, stoves, pots and pans, milk pails, lamps, axes, guns, and even flyswatters. Often saddles and harnesses were hanging on the wall.

In still another part of the store, shelves were filled with cloth, shoes, and clothing. On strings of wire overhead were stocking caps and mufflers. The general store might sell dishes, glassware, medicines, paper, and a few books.

General stores began doing business very early. Sometimes they opened at five o'clock in the morning. They stayed open until the last customer left in the evening.

The general store was more than just a store. It was also a place where people could visit. The men often gathered around a wood- or coal-burning stove. They swapped stories and heard the

In larger cities department stores took the place of general stores. This drawing shows the first floor of an early Kansas City department store.

latest news. The women visited while they selected the things they needed.

The general store was important in small Missouri towns for many years. But the automobile changed things. With cars, people could travel to larger cities and towns to shop.

In the larger towns and cities grocery stores and department stores took the place of the general store. The department stores were in very large buildings. The William Barr Company was the first and largest department store in St. Louis. It filled an entire city block. It sold many different kinds of goods. There was a separate department for each kind of goods. Each department had its own salespeople. Department stores sold ready-made clothing in different sizes. They also sold furniture, household goods, and many other items.

The department stores used glass display cases, mirrors, and colorful decorations to bring shoppers to their stores. They also provided rest rooms and restaurants for their customers. Many of their customers were women. They did much of the shopping for the family.

SPORTS COME TO MISSOURI

Baseball was the most popular sport in Missouri after the Civil War. Nearly every town had a team. Nearby towns often became great rivals.

In a few large cities there were professional teams. Their players were paid to play. The St. Louis Cardinal baseball team was one of the first teams in the National League. The St. Louis Browns became one of the first teams in the American League. Many years later the Browns moved to Baltimore and became the Orioles.

High Schools, colleges, and universities also had sports teams. Football and basketball were popular sports. The University of Missouri organized its first football team in 1890. They played their first game against Washington University in St. Louis that year. The team became known as the Missouri Tigers.

The University of Missouri's first football team was formed in 1890.

State Historical Society of Missouri

New Words

exposition	machine	kerosene
engineer	licorice	invent
kindergarten	fertilizer	electricity
consumer		

Fill in the Blanks

On another sheet of paper, rewrite the following sentences. Fill each blank with the proper word.

1. ________ ________ invented the electric light bulb.

2. The fair in St. Louis was held to mark the one hundredth birthday of the ═══════ ═══════.

3. ═══════ ═══════ ═══════ ═══════ ═══════ was one of the most popular songs in 1904.

4. Most Americans traveled to the St. Louis fair by ═══════.

5. Missouri's great horse trainer was ═══════ ═══════.

6. ═══════ ═══════ built the first bridge across the Mississippi River at St. Louis.

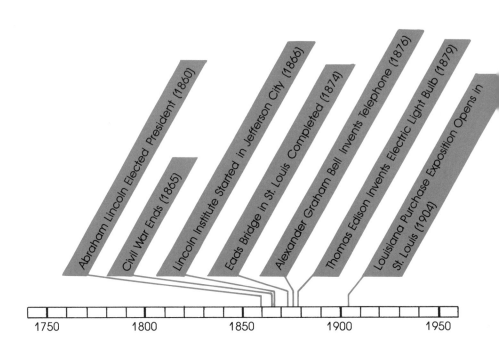

Abraham Lincoln Elected President (1860)

Civil War Ends (1865)

Lincoln Institute Started in Jefferson City (1866)

Eads Bridge in St. Louis Completed (1874)

Alexander Graham Bell Invents Telephone (1876)

Thomas Edison Invents Electric Light Bulb (1879)

Louisiana Purchase Exposition Opens in St. Louis (1904)

1750   1800   1850   1900   1950

Things to Do

1. Make a list of some things mentioned in this chapter that Missourians used to make their lives easier or better.

2. Draw several scenes of a factory or a farm.

3. Pretend that you are living in 1904. Write a letter inviting a friend to come to the St. Louis World's Fair. Describe some of the things your friend would be able to see there.

 # Things to Talk About

1. Why did more people move into cities during this time?

2. Before bridges were built, how did railroad cars get across rivers?

3. Did a railroad come to your town? What kinds of changes did it bring? Why are railroads less important today?

4. Does your city or town have any sports teams? What are their names?

 # Books You Can Read

Calhoun, Mary. *Ownself.* New York: Harper, 1975. (Fiction)

Draper, Cena Christopher. *Dandy and the Mystery of the Locked Room.* Independence, Mo.: Independence Press, 1974. (Fiction)

————. *Rim of the Ridge*. New York: Criterion, 1965. (Fiction)

————. *The Worst Hound Around*. Philadelphia: Westminster, 1979. (Fiction)

McCague, James. *When the Rails Ran West*. Champaign, Ill.: Garrard, 1967.

Martin, Patricia M. *Thomas Alva Edison*. New York: Putnam's, 1971.

Montgomery, Elizabeth R. *Alexander Graham Bell: Man of Sound*. Scarsdale, N.Y.: Garrard, 1963.

Myers, Hortense, and Ruth Burnett. *Joseph Pulitzer: Boy Journalist*. Indianapolis: Bobbs-Merrill, 1975.

Orrmont, Arthur. *James Buchanan Eads: The Man Who Mastered the Mississippi*. Englewood Cliffs, N.J.: Prentice-Hall, 1969.

Wilder, Laura Ingalls. *On the Way Home: The Diary of a Trip from South Dakota to Mansfield, Missouri in 1894*. New York: Harper, 1962.

Yeager, Rosemary. *James Buchanan Eads: Master of the Great River*. Princeton: Van Nostrand, 1968.

Chapter 14

GOOD TIMES AND BAD TIMES

Find the answers to these questions as you read.

What new weapons were used during World War I?

How did the automobile change people's lives?

What important changes for women happened during this time?

What was life like during the depression?

America had entered a new century. It was now the twentieth century. It was an exciting time. The world was changing. But the world was not always a happy and peaceful place. In 1914 a great world war began. Powerful new weapons like the submarine, the machine gun, and poison gas changed the way wars were fought. Many people died during World War I. After the war, the United States had a period of good times during the 1920s. It was called the Roaring Twenties. But the good times were followed by bad times. During the 1930s there was a Great Depression. Many people were out of work. The American people had to face many hardships.

WORLD WAR I COMES

A war started in Europe in 1914. Soon many nations were fighting. Great Britain, France, Russia, and other smaller nations were on one side. They were called the Allies. The other side was called the Central Powers. Germany, Austria-Hungary, Bulgaria, and Turkey were the Central Powers.

This war was known as the Great War because so many countries fought in it. Thousands of people were killed or injured. Later it was called World War I.

At first the United States stayed out of the war. Europe was far from the United States. The Atlantic Ocean was between them. Most Americans did not want their country to fight in the war. But it became harder and harder for the United States to stay out of the war. Some Americans believed that the Allied Powers were fighting for democracy. They did not want the Central Powers to win the war.

The German navy began to use a new weapon. It was a boat that could travel underwater. The Germans called these boats U-boats, but today we call them submarines. Sometimes these German U-boats sneaked up on ships and attacked them without warning. Some Americans lost their lives in those attacks.

President Woodrow Wilson of the United States asked Germany to stop the U-boat attacks. Germany did not. The United States declared war on Germany and the Central Powers. The United States became one of the Allied Powers.

MISSOURIANS HELP WIN THE WAR

The American people worked hard to win the Great War. The United States sent troops and supplies to Europe to help the Allies. Many Missourians joined the army and the navy. They fought in important battles of the war. A few Missouri women worked as volunteers in Red Cross canteens in Europe. The canteens provided soldiers with food, haircuts, and recreation.

Harry S. Truman was one of the many Missourians who went to

Harry S. Truman fought in Europe during World War I.

Harry S. Truman Library

Europe during World War I. Truman was born in Lamar, Missouri. He grew up in Jackson County and went to school in Independence. As a boy Truman loved to read. He enjoyed reading biographies of military leaders. General Robert E. Lee, the Confederate general, was one of Truman's heroes.

When he was young Truman decided that he wanted to be a soldier. Truman joined the Missouri National Guard and attended his first military training camp at Cape Girardeau. When the United States declared war on Germany in World War I, Truman's national guard unit went to France. Truman was captain of Company D. The men in Company D liked and respected "Captain Harry." Truman and his men fought in some big battles in France. After he returned to Missouri, Truman decided to run for public office. Many of "Captain Harry's" soldiers voted for him. Truman later became president of the United States.

Missourians are also proud of General John J. Pershing. He was

John J. Pershing

State Historical Society of Missouri

General John J. Pershing was one of Missouri's most famous soldiers. John Pershing grew up on a farm near Laclede. He liked living on a farm. He loved to ride horses.

After John graduated from high school, he wanted to go to college. But his family did not have enough money. John became a schoolteacher. Schools then often hired teachers with only high school diplomas. In his spare time Pershing helped with the farmwork.

Young Pershing still dreamed of going to college. One day he read about the United States Military Academy at West Point. It trained young men to become army officers. The school even paid students to attend. John was not sure he wanted to be a soldier. But he did want to go to college. Pershing wrote the school a letter and was invited to enter the Academy.

Pershing studied hard at West Point. He liked it very much. He soon decided that he wanted to make the army his career. When he graduated from West Point, he chose to serve in the cavalry. He

the commander of all American troops in Europe. Pershing was born and grew up in Laclede, Missouri. He went to the United States Military Academy at West Point. After graduating, he began his career as an army officer. Tourists can now visit Pershing's boyhood home in Laclede.

had always loved horses and was a good rider.

As a soldier, Pershing traveled to many different places. He served in the western part of the United States. He also held posts in Cuba, the Philippine Islands, Russia, and Mexico. Pershing was a good and brave officer. His men liked him. Because he was a good soldier, he earned many promotions. He became a general.

The United States entered World War I in 1917. Pershing was called to Washington, D.C. The secretary of war wanted Pershing to lead the American army in Europe. It was a big job, but Pershing was ready for it.

Pershing went to work at once. The United States army was not large. New soldiers had to be trained. General Pershing made sure that his soldiers were ready to fight. He did not send them into battle until they had been well trained. American soldiers fought bravely in many important battles.

General Pershing was a great soldier, but he did not like war. He did not like killing and suffering. He wanted to lose as few lives as possible.

When he returned to the United States, he was a great hero. Congress made him general of the armies. Only George Washington had been given that high rank before. Pershing had come a long way from the small Missouri farm.

Missourians helped win the war in other ways. Missouri farmers raised extra food to help feed America and its allies in Europe. Families tried not to waste anything. They raised vegetable gardens to provide more food. Many Missourians ate less sugar and meat. They wanted to send everything they could to Europe

John Pershing lived in this house when he was a boy in Laclede.

to support the war.

Workers in Missouri's factories produced clothing, shoes, chemicals, weapons, machinery, and other things needed to fight the war. Missourians also bought war bonds to help pay for the war.

The war finally ended in 1918. The Allies won the war with America's help. The Americans celebrated the victory. They hoped this war would be the last war that Americans would have to fight. Unfortunately it was not. The Liberty Memorial in Kansas City was built to honor the people who lost their lives during World War I.

LIFE IN THE 1920s

The Great War was over. Americans wanted things to be the way they had been before the war. The 1920s were good times for most Missourians. Most people had jobs. Many could afford to

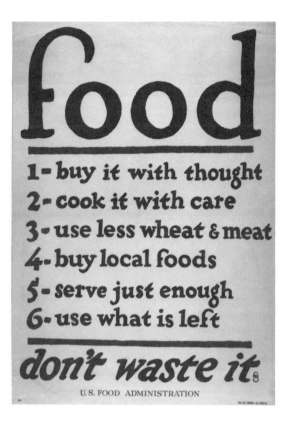

This World War I poster asked Americans not to waste food.

food

1 - buy it with thought
2 - cook it with care
3 - use less wheat & meat
4 - buy local foods
5 - serve just enough
6 - use what is left

don't waste it.

U.S. FOOD ADMINISTRATION

buy refrigerators, toasters, irons, phonographs, radios, and other new appliances.

Many Americans also bought their first automobile during the 1920s. Henry Ford had found a way to make cars that did not cost so much. He used an assembly line of workers to put them together. A Model T Ford sold for less than three hundred dollars. Many families could afford to own one.

Missourians wanted better roads for their new automobiles. Missouri passed a new law providing for a state highway system. This was the law that some people said "lifted Missouri out of the mud." Within a few years Missouri had many new paved roads.

Automobiles made it possible for people to travel more. This led to the establishment of new businesses for the travelers. Filling stations (service stations) sold gasoline, oil, and tires. Cafes (restaurants) and tourist cabins (motels) were also built along the new highways. Missouri organized the State Highway Patrol during the 1920s.

Some Missourians traveled to one of the new state parks. In the 1920s Missouri started its state park system. At first there were only seven state parks. Today Missouri has more than seventy state parks and historic sites. Millions of people visit them each year.

Missourians also listened to the radio for information and for entertainment. Missouri's first radio station was WEW in St. Louis. It began broadcasting in 1921. Before long other stations were on the air in St. Louis, Kansas City, Jefferson City, and Columbia.

Missourians found other new ways to enjoy themselves during the 1920s. They went to the movies. The first motion pictures were "silent pictures." They did not have sound. The words were printed on the screen. The people read the words to learn what the actors were saying. Most theaters hired a person to play a piano or organ during the movie. Sound was added during the late 1920s. Motion pictures with sound were called "talking pictures." The movies became so popular that large theaters had to be built to hold the people. The Midland Theater in Kansas City and the Fox Theater in St. Louis were two famous movie palaces. These beautiful theaters each had several thousand seats.

THE CHANGING ROLE OF WOMEN

The 1920s brought important changes for women. More women were working outside their homes. Most of them worked as teachers, nurses, secretaries, bookkeepers, store clerks, waitresses, and hairdressers. Missouri women also worked on farms and in factories. A few women like Nellie Peters moved into jobs that were usually held by men. Peters became an important architect in Kansas City. There were still many jobs that were not open to most women.

Women in Missouri had not been able to vote or hold office before 1920. In that year they won the right to vote. Many Missouri women voted in the elections. They helped elect the first women members of the Missouri General Assembly in 1923.

Emily Newell Blair was one of many Missouri women who worked to get more women involved in politics. She helped found the League of Women Voters in the 1920s. Later she became an active member of the Democratic party. She encouraged women to take an active part in politics and to run for office.

CHARLES A. LINDBERGH AND THE AIRPLANE

On May 20, 1927, many Americans stayed close to their radios. They were waiting to hear news of Charles A. Lindbergh. He was trying to fly his small one-engine airplane from New York to Paris, France, without stopping. This does not sound unusual today. But in 1927 no person had ever flown across the Atlantic Ocean alone.

Charles Lindbergh's plane was called the *Spirit of St. Louis*.

Lindbergh carried five sandwiches and two canteens of water with him. He named his plane the *Spirit of St. Louis*. He called it that because some people in St. Louis had given him the money he needed to make the flight.

Suddenly word came over the radio. Lindbergh had landed in Paris. It had taken him thirty-three hours and thirty minutes to make the thirty-six-hundred-mile trip. Lindbergh became a world hero. He received gifts and honors from many countries. Lindbergh and his family later gave many of those special gifts to the History Museum in Forest Park in St. Louis. They are on display there now.

Lindbergh's flight created great new interest in air travel. St. Louis leaders worked hard to promote flying. They made their city a major center for airplanes and flying.

LIFE IN THE 1930s

Not everyone had an easy time in the 1920s. Farmers found it hard to make a good living. Still, most Americans believed that the 1920s were good times. Then in 1929, things changed.

Business became bad all over the country. Factories stopped running. People lost their jobs and could not find new ones. Farmers received very low prices for their crops. Sometimes they could not find anyone to buy them at all. Many families did not have money to buy food. Hungry people had to stand in line for free meals. Some could not pay their rent. They were homeless. Few Missourians had money to buy new cars or radios. Such bad times are called a depression.

The depression seemed to get worse and worse. Since no one was buying, there was no need for factories to make things to sell. More factories and stores had to close. More workers lost their jobs. Many banks failed. People lost the money they had put in the banks. These were very hard times.

The national government tried to help the people. The job was a big one. The government put people without jobs to work. Workers hired by the government repaired old roads and built new

During the Great Depression these workers were put to work building sidewalks in St. Louis.

Art Witman photograph; courtesy State Historical Society of Missouri

ones. They made new parks and playgrounds. They built new post offices, city halls, courthouses, and school buildings. Young people were put to work planting trees and building dams. Some students got part-time jobs at schools and colleges. This allowed them to stay in school.

The government helped keep more banks from closing. It loaned money to companies to help them stay in business. It also gave help to farmers. Slowly things began to get better. The lives of the people started to improve.

THE HUNGRY YEARS: A MISSOURI FAMILY AND THE DEPRESSION

Thomas and Lulah May and their children lived in Adair County in northeast Missouri. The years of the depression were very hard for the Mays. Tom was a farm worker. He earned one dollar a day or less. Because of the depression he could not find work much of the time. The Mays had very little money to spend. Often they did not have enough to eat.

The only groceries that they bought during those years were flour, sugar, salt, dry beans, baking powder, lard, coffee, vinegar, and cocoa. They had to provide everything else they ate. Because they lived in the country, Tom and his boys could go hunting and fishing. Fish, squirrels, rabbits, wild ducks, and frogs were the main kinds of meat they had to eat. In the summer the Mays raised a big garden. In the spring they ate wild mushrooms, dandelions, and other wild plants.

Lulah canned vegetables, fruit, and meat in glass jars so they would have some food in the winter. One winter their house was so cold that the jars of food she had canned froze. That caused the jars to break.

The Mays could not afford to buy new clothes. Lulah sewed all of the family's clothes. Often she made them from used clothes that other people had given them. They bought their shoes from a Sears and Roebuck catalog. The children had only homemade toys. They made dolls and stuffed animals from socks. They used buttons for the eyes. They also made toys from wooden thread spools.

Cleo was the Mays' oldest child. When he was sixteen, he went to work for the Civilian Conservation Corps. It was a government program that hired young boys to work. He worked making dams and building roads. Each month the government gave him five dollars to keep. The government also sent twenty-five dollars every month to Cleo's family. Some months that was the only money the May family received. The work was hard. The boys in the CCC camp wore old World War I uniforms. Cleo was homesick some of the time, but he was glad to have a job during the depression.

Not all of the times were sad for the Mays. They did have good times. Tom liked to play the fiddle. They sometimes went to dances. There were also dinners and picnics with their relatives and friends. There were also special events at the one-room school that the May children attended. Friends and neighbors also helped them out sometimes.

Later the family moved from the country to Kirksville. Times were changing. World War II had started in Europe. In 1941 the United States went to war. Tom May was able to find a job. Cleo joined the Coast Guard and fought during the war. So did some of his younger brothers. Many years later, their sister Rowena wrote a book about her family and the depression. She called it *The Hungry Years*.

BLACK MISSOURIANS DURING THE DEPRESSION

The depression was also hard on black Missourians. African-Americans had always been given the worst jobs. With so many people out of work, it was even harder for them to find a job. They tried to make sure that they got their share of the new government jobs.

Missouri was different in one way from most other states that once had slavery. Black Missourians were allowed to vote after 1870. In 1921 Missouri voters elected the first black member of the Missouri General Assembly. Blacks could vote in Missouri, but Missouri was still a segregated state. There were separate schools for blacks. African-Americans could not stay in most hotels. Most restaurants served only whites.

During this time Missouri blacks worked to get these things changed. Lloyd Gaines asked the courts to let him attend the University of Missouri. Gaines had graduated from Lincoln University. He wanted to become a lawyer. There were no law schools in Missouri open to blacks. Gaines did not get to attend the University of Missouri. But his case was an important one for later African-Americans seeking equal treatment. Lucille Bluford was another black Missourian who helped in the fight to end segregation. Gaines and Bluford were early leaders in the civil rights movement.

HAVING FUN DURING THE 1930s

The depression was hard on most Missourians. But during these bad times they did find some ways to have fun. Missourians went to the movies. They enjoyed them, and many people could afford them. Movies were cheap. Some theaters charged as little as ten cents on some nights.

Missourians also watched baseball, basketball, and football games. Those who could not go to the games listened to them on the radio. The St. Louis Cardinals won the World Series in 1931 and 1934. The 1934 Cardinals team was known as the "Gas House Gang."

Black players could not play on white teams. They had to form their own leagues. The Kansas City Monarchs baseball team won

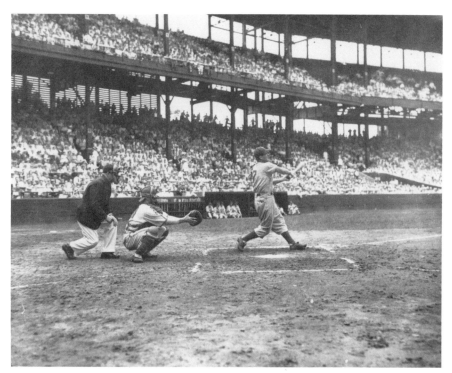

The St. Louis Cardinals defeated the Detroit Tigers in the 1934 World Series.

Charles Trefts photograph; courtesy State Historical Society of Missouri

William "Count" Basie played jazz in Kansas City during the 1930s.

Willard Alexander, Inc., N.Y.

the Negro American League pennant in 1937, 1939, and 1940. In 1941 the great black pitcher Satchel Paige began pitching for the Monarchs. He was one of baseball's greatest pitchers. Sports writers later chose him to be in the Baseball Hall of Fame.

Football was also a popular sport. Paul Christman played football for the University of Missouri Tigers during the 1930s. He became Missouri's first all-American football player.

Missourians listened and danced to the music played by famous bands. Kansas City and St. Louis had become famous in the 1920s for their jazz. During the 1930s jazz players from all over the country came to Kansas City. Kansas City jazz was black music. It was played by black musicians like William "Count" Basie.

☛ New Words

submarine	victory	depression
commander	theater	cavalry
bonds	conservation	jazz
architect		

Testing Yourself

1. The United States wanted to stay out of World War I. But Germany made many Americans angry. What did Germany do?

2. How did Missourians help win World War I?

3. What new inventions helped people have fun in the 1920s?

4. What made Charles Lindbergh a hero?

5. What problems did people have during the depression?

6. What did the government do to put people to work during the depression?

7. What group of people gained the right to vote in the 1920s?

8. What did Lloyd Gaines do that was important?

 # Things to Talk About

1. Have you visited any of Missouri's state parks? Which ones? Which state park did you like best? Why?

2. How would a depression today change your life?

 # Things to Do

1. Talk to someone who lived during the Great Depression. Ask them to tell you what it was like. Tell the class what you learned.

Matching Partners

Match the right partners. Use another sheet of paper.

1. Germany

2. Charles A. Lindbergh

3. John J. Pershing

4. Satchel Paige

5. Great Britain

a. flew the *Spirit of St. Louis*

b. commander of American army in Europe during World War I

c. fought on the same side as the United States in World War I

d. fought against the United States during World War I

e. famous baseball pitcher

 # Choose the Right Words

Select the right words to finish each of the following sentences. Write each sentence correctly on another sheet of paper.

1. During World War I, Great Britain, France, Russia, and the United States were called the (Allies, Central Powers).

2. During World War I, Germany, Austria-Hungary, Bulgaria, and Turkey were called the (Allies, Central Powers).

3. One reason the United States joined the war was because the Germans attacked many ships with their (U-boats, airplanes).

4. The Model T Ford was an early (automobile, airplane, bicycle).

Books You Can Read

Bachmann, Evelyn Trent. *Black-Eyed Susan.* New York: Viking, 1968. (Fiction)

Colby, C. B. *Fighting Gear of World War One.* New York: Coward, McCann and Geoghegan, 1961.

Collins, David R. *Charles Lindbergh: Hero Pilot.* New York: Chelsea House, 1991.

Devaney, John. *The Greatest Cardinals of Them All.* New York: Putnam's, 1968.

Foster, John. *John J. Pershing: World War I Hero.* Champaign, Ill.: Garrard, 1970.

Phelan, Joseph. *Aeroplanes and Flyers of the First World War.* New York: Grosset and Dunlap, 1973.

Pope, Rowena May. *The Hungry Years.* Circle Pines, Minn.: Bold Blue Jay Publications, 1982.

Potter, Marian. *Blatherskite.* New York: Morrow, 1980. (Fiction)

————. *Milepost 67.* Chicago: Follett, 1965. (Fiction)

Rabe, Berniece. *Orphans.* New York: Dutton, 1978. (Fiction)

————. *Rass.* New York: Nelson, 1973. (Fiction)

Rubin, Robert. *Satchel Paige: All-Time Baseball Great.* New York: Putnam's, 1974.

Snyder, Louis. *The First Book of World War I.* New York: Franklin Watts, 1958.

Stein, R. Conrad. *The Story of the Great Depression.* Chicago: Childrens Press, 1985.

————. *The Story of the Spirit of St. Louis.* Chicago: Childrens Press, 1984.

Chapter 15

MISSOURIANS IN THE MODERN WORLD

Find the answers to these questions as you read.

What event caused the United States to declare war on the Axis Powers in World War II?

Who was known as "the man from Missouri"?

What kinds of changes did leaders in the civil rights movement want?

Americans had hoped that World War I would be the last war. Leaders from different countries worked to bring peace to the world. But the peace did not last long. Another war began only a few years after World War I ended. It was known as World War II.

HOW WORLD WAR II BEGAN

There were many reasons for World War II. Leaders called dictators took over the governments in Germany, Italy, and Japan. These dictators wanted to control everything. The people in their countries had little freedom. The dictators built large armies. They used their armies to take over other countries. The leaders in Germany, Italy, and Japan agreed to help each other. Those three countries became known as the Axis Powers.

World War II began when Germany attacked Poland in 1939. England and France tried to help Poland. They went to war against Germany. Later the Union of Soviet Socialist Republics (Russia) agreed to fight with England and France against the Axis countries. England, France, and Russia called themselves the Allies.

Just as in World War I, most Americans hoped to stay out of the war. Still, they wanted the Allies to win. The Americans did not trust Adolf Hitler. He was the German dictator. He was mean and cruel. He ordered the killing of many Jews. The United States sent ships and guns to the Allies to help them defeat Hitler.

But something happened that forced the United States to declare war on the Axis Powers. In December 1941 Japanese airplanes dropped bombs on the United States military base at Pearl Harbor in Hawaii. Japan was on the same side as Germany. The Japanese bombs sank many American ships at Pearl Harbor. Hundreds of Americans were killed in the attack. The United States Congress declared war on Japan and the other Axis countries.

MISSOURIANS HELP WIN THE WAR

Nearly one-half million men and women from Missouri served in the American armed forces during World War II. Over eight thousand Missourians were killed in the fighting. Many others suffered wounds that left them permanently disabled.

Lieutenant George Whiteman was the first Missourian to be killed in the fighting during World War II. He was a pilot who was killed during the attack on Pearl Harbor. Whiteman Air Force Base at Knob Noster was named for this Missouri war hero.

General Omar N. Bradley from Randolph County, Missouri, was an outstanding military leader. He was very popular with the sol-

Many African-American soldiers fought in World War II.

Painting by Thomas Hart Benton; courtesy State Historical Society of Missouri

diers. Bradley became one of America's most respected generals.

Captain Wendell Pruitt of St. Louis was one of the first African-American pilots in the U.S. Army Air Corps. He flew many missions in Italy and won many medals for his bravery. He was later killed during a training flight in the United States.

Missourians at home helped win the war, too. Farmers produced extra corn, wheat, oats, cotton, soybeans, and livestock. Some city boys and girls spent summers on farms to help with the farm work.

Missouri's mines provided iron, lead, and zinc. These minerals were used in making weapons and other goods. Workers in Missouri factories made airplanes, tanks, guns, bullets, chemicals, trucks, machinery, and medical supplies. They also made uniforms and shoes for the people in the armed forces. Many Missouri factories changed what they made. Automobile factories

President Harry Truman congratulates General Omar Bradley while General George Marshall looks on. Both Truman and Bradley were from Missouri.

stopped making cars and started making airplanes or tanks.

Before the war, only a few Missouri women held jobs outside the home. With many workers fighting the war, someone had to take their places. Thousands of women went to work in all kinds of jobs. They took over jobs that only men had done before the war. They did them well.

Missourians bought war bonds to help pay for the war. Thousands of young Missourians saved their allowances to buy bonds. Americans also tried not to waste anything. Children collected newspapers, scrap metal, and grease. These products were recycled and used to make things needed to fight the war.

Fort Leonard Wood in Pulaski County was one of the army's largest training camps. Soldiers from all over the United States trained there. Some soldiers also trained at Jefferson Barracks near St. Louis. Others trained at Camp Crowder near Neosho and

During World War II more women worked in factories than ever before. This woman worked in a Missouri airplane factory.

Western Historical Manuscripts Collection, University of Missouri–St. Louis

Fort Leonard Wood in Pulaski County was one of the army's largest training camps during World War II.

State Historical Society of Missouri

World War II ended when Japanese leaders signed the surrender on the USS *Missouri*.

Harry S. Truman Library

Harry S. Truman became president of the United States in 1945.

Harry S. Truman Library

on the campuses of Missouri's colleges and universities. Pilots were also trained at the Sedalia Army Air Field. It later became White-man Air Force Base.

World War II was a long and hard fight. The Allies finally won, four years after the United States entered the war. Japan was the last Axis nation to surrender. The war ended when Japanese leaders signed the surrender on the battleship USS *Missouri*. Missourians could be proud of their part in winning the war.

THE MAN FROM MISSOURI BECOMES PRESIDENT

Franklin D. Roosevelt was the president of the United States during most of World War II. But a short time before the war ended, President Roosevelt died. Vice-President Harry S. Truman became the new president.

Harry Truman was the first Missourian to become president of the United States. He faced a very difficult task. He had to lead the country through the last months of the war. He also had to be a world leader. The United States was the richest and most powerful nation in the world. Truman did a fine job. In 1948 the American voters elected Truman to serve as president for four more years. Many people consider Truman one of America's great presidents. After his term as president was over, Truman came back to his home in Independence. His friends built a library and museum in Independence to honor Missouri's only president.

THE UNITED STATES AS A WORLD POWER

The United States is a global power. Since World War II it has sent troops to many parts of the world to help keep the peace. American men and women took part in two wars in Asia. One was fought in Korea. The Korean War began when Harry Truman was president. It ended in 1953. The other Asian war was fought in Vietnam. The United States had military advisers and soldiers in

FAMOUS MISSOURIANS

Harry S. Truman Library

Harry S. Truman

On April 12, 1945, Harry S. Truman placed his hand on a Bible and promised that he would "pre serve, protect, and defend" the United States Con stitution. With those words Truman became the thirty-third president of the United States. He wa the first Missourian to hold that high office. "Th man from Missouri" became one of America's gre leaders.

Truman was born in the small Missouri town o Lamar. When Truman was young, his family moved to Independence. He went to school there

As a boy, Harry loved to read. By the time he was thirteen he had read every book in his home town library. History books were his favorites. H especially liked to read biographies of great per sons. For the rest of his life, Truman was inter ested in history. Truman believed his study of history helped him as president.

When Truman graduated from high school, he went to work. He held several different jobs. He worked for a railroad, a bank, and a newspaper. Truman next moved to Grandview to run his grandmother's farm.

Truman joined the Missouri National Guard. When the United States entered World War I, the Missouri National Guard was sent to fight in Eu rope. Truman was chosen to be an officer. He wa a good leader and was popular with his men.

After the war Truman decided not to go back to the farm. Instead he opened a clothing store in Kansas City with a friend. The business failed, and Truman decided to run for public office. He was elected to serve on the Jackson County Court He was a good county official. He was honest an worked very hard. His good work in running the government in Jackson County made him popular with the people. They later elected him a United States senator from Missouri.

Truman was a good senator. In 1944 President Franklin D. Roosevelt asked him to run for vice-president of the United States. Truman was elected. When President Roosevelt died very suddenly in 1945, Truman became president. Roosevelt's death was a shock to Truman. Truman worried about whether he would be able to handle such a big job. So did many other Americans. The United States had many problems to solve. World War II was still going on.

The job was not too big for Harry Truman. He took charge. He led the United States through the last months of World War II. He helped start the United Nations. He helped the world make the change from a time of war to a time of peace. He started many programs to help the people whose countries had been destroyed by the war. He also worked to make things better for the American people.

Truman became a great world leader, but he did not lose his love for Missouri. He was still "the man from Missouri." He knew how to talk to people. They listened to what he had to say. Most of them liked Harry Truman. The American people elected Truman to serve four more years as president.

After his term as president was over, Truman came back to his home in Independence. The Harry S. Truman Library is also in Independence. It contains many important papers from the years when Truman was president. It also has a museum that tells the story of the Truman presidency. Truman is buried in the garden of the library. Each year thousands of visitors from all parts of the world visit the Truman Library and the Truman home.

Truman's birthplace at Lamar is a state historic site. It is another interesting place to visit in Missouri.

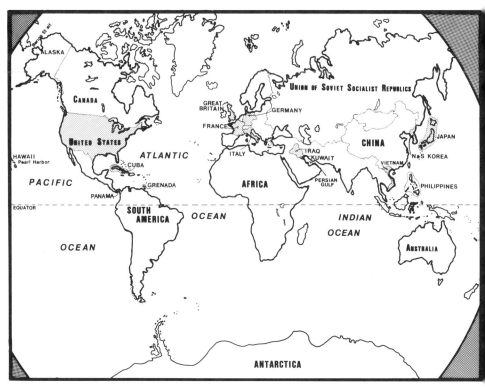

The World in 1990. What changes have occurred since then?

Vietnam for nearly fifteen years. The Vietnam War was the longest war the United States ever fought.

Missourians fought and died in both the Korean and Vietnam wars. General Maxwell Taylor of Keytesville was a World War II hero who also served in Korea and in Vietnam. During the Vietnam War there were some Americans who did not think that the United States should be fighting there. They protested against the war. The United States withdrew its last soldiers from Vietnam in 1975.

During the 1980s the United States sent its troops to Panama and Grenada. Panama is a county in Central America. The Panama Canal is located there. Grenada is a small island in the Caribbean.

In 1991 the United States also fought a war in the Persian Gulf region in the Middle East. It began after soldiers from Iraq took over the country of Kuwait. Women and men in the United States Armed Forces joined with troops from many other nations to force the Iraqi soldiers to leave Kuwait. The actual fighting lasted only a few days. The War in the Persian Gulf was the shortest war the United States ever fought. Many Missourians took part in this war. The battleship USS *Missouri* was used once again in the Persian Gulf War.

THE CIVIL RIGHTS MOVEMENT

Wars were not America's only problem. Almost one hundred years after the Civil War ended slavery in the United States African-Americans still did not have equal rights.

In Missouri black people could vote, but they had to attend all-black schools. Those schools were not as good as the white schools. Laws also prevented black Missourians from going to many restaurants, hotels, theaters, parks, and other places. This

Civil rights demonstrators blocked traffic in downtown St. Louis in the early 1960s.

From the St. Louis Globe-Democrat *Photograph Collection of the St. Louis Mercantile Library Association*

FAMOUS MISSOURIANS

Lucile H. Bluford

Columbia Missourian,
photographer Hal Wells

In 1939 Lucile Bluford traveled to Columbia, Missouri, where she wanted to study at the state university. Bluford had graduated from the University of Kansas. But she wanted to study journalism at the University of Missouri. It was famous for its School of Journalism.

There was one problem. Lucile Bluford was black. At that time the University of Missouri was not open to African-Americans. It was segregated. Lucile was not allowed to become a student there.

She believed this was wrong. She believed her rights had been taken away. She was an American citizen. She was a good student. She believed that she should be able to go to the university. She asked the courts to make the university allow her to attend classes there. At that time the civil rights movement was not popular with most Americans.

was known as segregation. African-Americans could not get good jobs. Many companies would not hire them because they were black.

Blacks in America said that these things had to change. They worked to end segregation. They wanted to have the same rights as white Americans. This was called the civil rights movement. Many white Americans also joined the civil rights movement.

In 1954 the United States Supreme Court said that segregation was wrong. Later the United States Congress passed new laws to give all Americans the same rights. In 1957 Missouri leaders cre-

It took a brave person to do what Lucile Bluford did.

She did not get to attend the university. But what Lucile Bluford did was important. It was a big step in the movement to win equal treatment for all Americans. Later the United States Supreme Court said that segregation was wrong.

Bluford was a leader in the civil rights movement. The governor chose her to be one of the first members of the Missouri Commission on Human Rights. She was a leader in the National Association for the Advancement of Colored People, too.

She became a very good newspaperwoman. For many years she was editor of the *Kansas City Call*. Bluford was also active in community affairs. Fifty years after Bluford tried to enroll at the University of Missouri, that school gave her an honorary doctor's degree. That is the highest kind of degree that the university can give. The University of Missouri gives that award only to very distinguished people. It was a well-deserved honor for a woman who worked in many different ways to win equal treatment for all Americans.

ated a Commission on Human Rights. Its job is to see that all Missourians are treated fairly and have the same chance for jobs. Civil rights leaders organized groups to protest the unfair treatment of black people in America.

Ivory Perry was an African-American who joined the protest movement. He had come to St. Louis after the Korean War. Many times in his life he had been treated unfairly because he was black. Perry was not famous. He was an ordinary person who thought he should try to do something to make things better for black people. He marched and carried signs calling for an end to segregation. He sat down in doorways of companies that did not hire black workers. He blocked traffic to remind people of the problems of black Americans.

Perry's acts made some people angry. He suffered many hardships. He sometimes became discouraged. Things did not change as fast as Perry hoped they would. But he kept on working to do what he could to make things better for African-Americans. His story is an important one. It reminds us that there is still much to be done before all Americans are treated the same and have equal rights.

THE WOMEN'S MOVEMENT

Blacks were not the only group to protest because they did not have equal rights. Women also did not receive equal treatment. After World War II, more and more American women went to work outside their homes. They held almost every type of job. They began forming organizations to work for equal treatment and equal pay. In Missouri these organizations included the National Organization for Women (NOW), the League of Women Voters, the American Association of University Women, and the Business and Professional Women's Association.

Women began to move into leadership positions in government, business, industry, and other fields. Leonor Sullivan became the first woman to be elected to the United States House of Representatives from Missouri. She served in Congress for twenty-four years. She became well known for supporting laws to protect consumers. Harriet Woods was elected lieutenant governor of Missouri, and Margaret Kelly was elected state auditor.

A TIME OF PROTESTS

There were other kinds of protests during the 1970s and the 1980s. Many Missourians worried about the environment. They worked to get clean air and clean water. Some were afraid of the dangers of nuclear power. Other Missourians worried about poor and homeless people. They sometimes marched carrying signs to show that they were unhappy with the way things were. Not everyone agreed with the protesters. But the United States Bill of Rights protects the right of protesters to say what they believe.

 # New Words

peace	judge	commission
museum	dictator	recycle
nuclear	Jews	barracks

 # Things to Talk About

1. Today many more women are in the work force than ever before. How many different jobs are held by mothers of students in your class?

2. Do you think we will have a woman president soon?

3. World leaders hoped that World War I would be the last war. Sadly, it was not. After World War II, nations formed the United Nations. The United Nations was formed to solve disagreements among nations without war. Do you think it has worked?

 # Testing Yourself

1. What countries were the Axis Powers?

2. What countries were the Allies?

3. Name some famous military leaders from Missouri.

4. Who was the only Missourian to become president of the United States?

5. What did Missourians do to help win World War II?

6. Name the three wars that Americans have fought in since World War II.

7. What things did civil rights leaders do to bring about changes?

8. What is the Missouri Commission on Human Rights?

 Things to Do

1. On a map of the world locate the following places:
   a. Pearl Harbor, Hawaii
   b. Japan
   c. Italy
   d. England
   e. France
   f. U.S.S.R.
   g. Vietnam
   h. Korea
   i. Iraq
   j. Persian Gulf

2. Talk to your parents, grandparents, or any other adults who remember World War II, the Korean War, the Vietnam War, or the War in the Persian Gulf. Ask them to tell you some of the things that they remember about the war. Write down some of those things and share them with members of your class.

Using a Time Line

1. Put these events in the proper order on another sheet of paper.
   American Forces Fight in the Persian Gulf
   War in Vietnam Ends
   Louisiana Purchase Exposition Is Held
   Great Depression Begins
   The United States Enters World War II

2. Study the time line on this page to see the years that Harry Truman lived. Could he have gone to the world's fair in St. Louis?

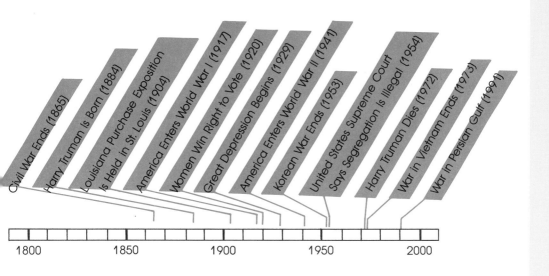

Civil War Ends (1865)
Harry Truman Is Born (1884)
Louisiana Purchase Exposition Is Held in St. Louis (1904)
America Enters World War I (1917)
Women Win Right to Vote (1920)
Great Depression Begins (1929)
America Enters World War II (1941)
Korean War Ends (1953)
United States Supreme Court Says Segregation Is Illegal (1954)
Harry Truman Dies (1972)
War in Vietnam Ends (1973)
War in Persian Gulf (1991)

1800   1850   1900   1950   2000

Books You Can Read

Collins, David R. *Harry S. Truman: People's President*. New York: Chelsea House, 1991.

Hargrove, Jim. *Harry S. Truman*. Chicago: Childrens Press, 1987.

Leavell, J. Perry, Jr. *Harry S. Truman*. New York: Chelsea House, 1988.

McKissack, Patricia, and Frederick McKissack. *The Civil Rights Movement in America from 1865 to the Present*. Chicago: Childrens Press, 1987.

Reeder, Red (Russell P. Jr.). *Omar Nelson Bradley: The Soldiers' General*. Champaign, Ill.: Garrard, 1969.

Sutton, Felix. *How and Why Wonder Book of World War 2*. New York: Wonder-Treasure Books, 1962.

Chapter 16

GOVERNMENT IN MISSOURI

Find the answers to these questions as you read.

Why do we need laws?

What is a democracy?

What kinds of things do governments do?

How does a government get its money?

Long ago people learned that they needed rules in order to live together. Rules can do many things. They can help prevent conflicts between people. They can provide for people's safety and welfare. They can protect people's rights. Without rules, there would be many more problems. Each person would be free to do whatever she or he wanted. They might do things that would hurt other people. They might not respect the rights of others.

Governments were set up to make rules and to make sure that everyone follows the rules. These rules are known as laws. Can you give some examples of different kinds of laws that we have today? What would happen if we did not have these laws?

Governments do more than pass laws. They also provide many services for people. They operate armies and navies. They build roads and bridges. They establish and run schools. Governments allow people to work together to do things that it would be difficult for them to do by themselves. What other services can you name that governments provide for the people?

DIFFERENT KINDS OF GOVERNMENT

There have been many different kinds of government. Long ago most countries were ruled by a king or a queen. These rulers were members of a special family that claimed the right to run the country. People became kings and queens only because they were born into those families. The king or queen of a country made the laws. The people had to obey the laws.

Today some countries are ruled by dictators. The dictators also claim the right to make all laws. Dictators take control of a government by force. They expect the people in their countries to do what they say. They give the people few rights.

Democracy is another kind of government. A democracy is a government run by the people. In a democracy the people choose their rulers. They do this by holding elections. In a democracy the people have more rights. They also have responsibilities. In order for a democracy to work well, the citizens must take an interest in their government. They must learn about the problems that the government has to deal with. They must choose good leaders. They must see that their leaders rule fairly. They must also see that the government does not take the people's rights away from them. People who do these things are good citizens.

GOVERNMENT IN THE UNITED STATES

The government of the United States is a democracy. The American people elect their leaders. The United States has both a national government and fifty state governments. The national government is called the United States government. It makes laws and provides services for the whole country. It runs the army, navy, marines, and air force to protect us from foreign enemies. It makes treaties with other countries. It prints our paper money and makes our coins. It helps take care of old and needy people. It operates national parks. These are only a few of the things the United States government does.

The most important leader in the United States is the president. The president is in charge of the executive branch. The president enforces the laws. It is the president's job to see that the national laws are carried out and that the people obey them. The president lives in Washington, D.C. It is the capital city of the United States.

The United States Congress also meets in Washington, D.C. The Congress makes laws for the United States. It is the legislative branch of government. The citizens of each state elect people to represent them in Congress. The Congress is made up of two groups. One is called the United States House of Representatives, and the other is called the United States Senate.

The United States Supreme Court meets in Washington, D.C., too. It is the most important court in the United States. The Supreme Court helps explain what the laws mean. It interprets the laws. The courts are called the judicial branch.

The United States is a large country. It is divided into fifty states. Each state has its own government. Each state government takes

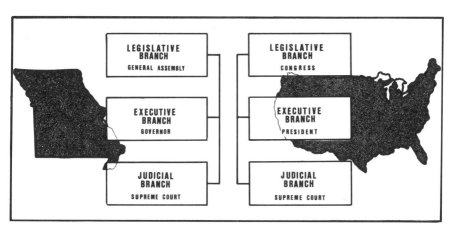

The Three Branches of Government.

FAMOUS MISSOURIANS

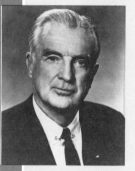

State Historical Society
of Missouri

Stuart Symington

Many people wanted Stuart Symington to be a candidate for president of the United States. Symington was a United States senator from Missouri. At the 1960 Democratic National Convention Symington's supporters asked the delegates to choose him to be their party's candidate. They made speeches telling why they thought he would be a good president. They carried banners saying "Symington for President." It was an exciting time for the Missouri senator.

Symington must have remembered his first political party convention. When he was ten years old, he had attended the 1912 Democratic National Convention. That convention had been held near his home in Baltimore. To earn money, he got a job selling gum, peanuts, candy, and Cracker Jacks to the delegates. But in the 1960 convention Symington was not selling Cracker Jacks. He was running for president. Symington did not win. The Democrats chose John F. Kennedy to be their candidate. But it had been a great honor for Symington to have been considered for the highest office in the land. He had come a long way since his boyhood.

care of many of the problems in the state. State governments operate schools. They also help take care of people with special problems. They build roads and bridges. They also pass laws to protect lives and property.

Symington was not born in Missouri. He was born in Massachusetts. He served in the army during World War I. After the war he graduated from Yale University. He became a successful businessman. He moved to St. Louis to run the Emerson Electric Manufacturing Company. Stuart Symington had become a Missourian.

At the end of World War II another Missourian, President Harry S. Truman, asked Symington to work for him in the government. Symington accepted Truman's offer. He later became the first secretary of the air force.

Symington returned to Missouri to run for the United States Senate. Missourians elected him to be their senator four times. As a senator Symington worked for equal rights for all Americans. He once canceled a speech that he was supposed to make when he learned that African-Americans would not be seated with the other guests. He supported Social Security and other government programs to help people. He also worked to have a strong military force to defend the United States.

Stuart Symington had a remarkable career. He was a successful businessman, government official, and politician. He was the kind of leader that all Americans, and especially Missourians, can be proud of.

STATE GOVERNMENT IN MISSOURI

Before Missouri became a state in the Union, the people chose representatives to write a constitution. A constitution tells the kind of officers a state will have. It also tells what these officers can do.

The Missouri Constitution protects the rights and freedoms of the people of Missouri. It keeps the leaders from doing anything they want. One important part of the constitution is the Bill of Rights. The Bill of Rights says that Missourians can go to any church they want. It protects their freedom of speech and the freedom of the press. The government cannot keep people from criticizing their leaders. The Bill of Rights also says that each person has the right to have a fair trial.

The Missouri Constitution divides the state government into three branches. They are the same as the three branches of the national government. One branch makes the laws. Another branch enforces the laws. The third branch interprets what the law means and helps settle disputes.

The Missouri General Assembly is the branch that makes the laws for the state. The people of Missouri elect the members of the

Members of the Missouri Senate conduct business in the state capitol.

Missouri State Senate

This is the governor's mansion in Jefferson City. When each governor is in office, he or she lives here.

Missouri Division of Tourism

General Assembly. The two parts of the General Assembly are the State House of Representatives and the State Senate. The General Assembly meets in Jefferson City. Jefferson City is the capital of the state of Missouri.

The governor is the main officer of the second branch of state government. The governor lives in Jefferson City. The people also elect the governor. He or she makes sure that the laws are carried out. There are many departments that help the governor do her or his job. One such department is the highway department. It helps build and take care of roads in Missouri. Another department is the department of elementary and secondary education. It helps run Missouri's schools.

The third branch of state government is made up of the courts. Disagreements between people are settled in a court. When a person is accused of breaking a law, the person is usually brought before a judge and a jury for a trial. A jury is a group of citizens. The jury and the judge decide whether or not the person has broken the law.

CITY GOVERNMENT

Each town in Missouri has a government of its own. Not all city governments are alike. But all towns do have a city council. The members of a city council are elected by the people in a city. The city council makes laws for the city. Most cities have a mayor. The mayor carries out the laws. Some cities have a city manager to help run the city.

Most city governments hire police officers and fire fighters to protect the people in the city and their property. Cities also build

COUNTIES OF MISSOURI

and take care of streets, sewers, and parks in the town. Sometimes a city will run a hospital or even a city animal shelter.

COUNTY GOVERNMENT

Missouri is divided into 114 counties, plus the city of St. Louis, which is considered a county. It is separate from St. Louis County. Some of the most important county leaders are the county commissioners, the sheriff, and the tax collector. The county governments provide for people who live outside the cities many of the same things that cities do for their residents.

There are several school districts in each county. Each school district also has a government. The voters in each school district elect several people to run the schools. They are members of the school board. The school board hires the teachers and others who help run the schools. It works to see that there are good school buildings. The board also makes many other decisions about how the schools operate.

HOW GOVERNMENTS GET MONEY

A government could do very little without money. The money comes from the people. The government gets its money mainly from taxes. Each citizen must pay taxes.

There are many different kinds of taxes. A sales tax is added to the price of things you buy. The stores send the tax money to the government. Another tax is the income tax. The more money a person earns, the more income tax the person usually pays. The property tax provides schools, libraries, cities, and counties with some of their money. There are many other taxes like gasoline and cigarette taxes.

Many people do not like to pay taxes. But citizens should remember that the taxes they pay help the government provide us with many things. At the same time it is important for citizens to make sure that their governments do not waste their tax money.

 **New Words**

jury	taxes	income tax
property tax	sales tax	county
Congress	mayor	

 Choose the Right Words

Select the right words in each of these sentences. Then re-write each sentence correctly on another sheet of paper.

1. The United States is made up of (forty, fifty) states.

2. The (court, general assembly) makes the laws in Missouri.

3. Missouri's main leader is called the (governor, president).

4. A group of citizens who help decide whether a person has broken a law is called a (jury, judge).

5. When you buy something at a store, you pay (an income, a sales) tax on your purchase.

6. The group of people who run a city is the (city council, general assembly).

✔ Testing Yourself

1. Why do we have governments?

2. Give examples of some of the laws that we have.

3. What are the three branches of government?

4. What are some of the things that the United States government does?

5. What are some of the things that the state government does?

6. What are some of the things that city and county governments do?

7. What are some different kinds of taxes that we have?

Things to Find Out

1. Who is the governor of Missouri?

2. Who is your state representative?

3. Who is your state senator?

4. Who is the mayor of your town or city?

5. Does your city or town have a city manager? If so, what is his or her name?

6. What is the name of your county? In what town do your county officials have their offices?

Things to Talk About

1. What would happen if we had no laws?

2. How do we choose our officials? What are political parties?

Things to Do

1. Make a list of all the things you can think of that Missouri governments do for people. How many of these things does your family use?

2. Have an election in your class. Decide who the candidates will be. Hold a rally with speeches and posters.

Chapter 17

MISSOURI TODAY

Find the answers to these questions as you read.

From what different parts of the world have many new people come to Missouri in recent times?

How has farming changed in Missouri?

What is manufacturing? How is manufacturing changing?

What are Missouri's important resources?

Why has tourism become an important Missouri industry?

How are today's schools different from the schools in early Missouri?

Since the end of World War II, Missouri has grown and changed. Many new people have come to the state. There have also been important changes in farming, manufacturing, mining, and other areas of life in Missouri.

TODAY'S MISSOURIANS

From the earliest times Missouri has always been a popular place for people to settle. People have come to Missouri from nearly all parts of the world. Missouri's first settlers were the Native Americans. People from Europe and Africa followed them to America. In recent times many new people from Asia and from the Spanish-speaking countries of North and South America have also come to Missouri.

FARMING TODAY

In the early years most Missourians lived and worked on farms. Today most Missourians live in cities and towns, but farming is still an important business in the state.

There are fewer Missouri farmers today, but they grow more food. The farms are larger, and most farmers use modern farm machinery. These machines do the work of many people.

Farmers plow fertilizer into the soil to make the plants produce more. Many farmers also use chemicals to kill weeds and insects. Today's farmers need special skills and knowledge to be successful. Chemicals must be used properly to protect the environment from pollution. Modern farmers must also practice conservation. Many Missouri farmers work hard to prevent wind and water erosion. They want to save the state's rich soil.

The University of Missouri has a College of Agriculture and an extension service that provide help for Missouri farmers. Even with all of the modern inventions farming is hard work.

Farming is also big business. Good farmland and modern farm machinery are very expensive. So are fertilizer and farm chemicals. When farmers receive low prices for their crops or when the crops are poor because of bad weather, farmers lose money. In good years they make money.

A combine harvests soybeans near Carrollton.

Missouri Farm Bureau Federation

Missouri farmers sometimes work together to deal with farm problems. Farmers own and operate some companies like the Missouri Farmers Association (known as MFA), Farmland Industries, and Mid-America Dairymen. Farmers also belong to farmers' organizations like the Missouri Farm Bureau and the National Farmers Organization.

Early Missouri farmers grew many different kinds of crops on their farms. Today most Missouri farmers raise only one or two crops. Corn, soybeans, wheat, and grain sorghum are important Missouri crops. Farmers in the Missouri bootheel grow cotton and rice. Missouri farmers are livestock producers too. They raise cattle, hogs, and poultry. Others have large dairy herds. Some Missouri farmers grow vegetables, fruit, and berries. Missourians sell their farm products throughout the world. Missouri ranks as one of the nation's leading farm states.

MANUFACTURING

Missouri is also a state with many factories. Many Missourians work in factories. They make many different kinds of products. Automobiles, airplanes, space vehicles, food items, chemicals, and electronic equipment are only a few of the products made in Missouri.

St. Louis is the state's most important manufacturing center. It is the home of many famous American companies. The McDonnell Douglas Corporation makes airplanes, spacecraft, military weapons, computers, and electronic equipment. The Monsanto Company is a large chemical company. Anheuser-Busch, Ralston Purina, and Southwestern Bell also have their headquarters in St. Louis.

The Kansas City skyline as it looks today.

Missouri Division of Tourism

FAMOUS MISSOURIANS

Joyce C. Hall

It was a cold winter day in January when eighteen-year-old Joyce C. Hall got off the train in Kansas City. Joyce was a man who never liked his first name. When he was growing up other boys sometimes teased him about having a girl's name. In later years he often used his initials, J. C.

Hall had come to Kansas City to start a business selling picture postcards. He had chosen Kansas City because a cigar salesman from there had told him that it was a place with hardworking people who got things done. He also chose Kansas City because it had a central location and many railroads.

Joyce Hall was born in Nebraska. The Halls were very poor. His father left when Joyce was young. Joyce Hall and his brothers had to go to work to support their family. Joyce was nine years old when he began selling perfume to make money. When his brothers bought a bookstore, he worked for them after school and on Saturdays. The Halls sold picture postcards in their store. The cards were very popular. Joyce Hall had to drop

Hallmark Cards

Kansas City also has many manufacturing plants. Kansas City's Hallmark Card Company is known all over the world for its greeting cards. Springfield, Columbia, and St. Joseph have smaller industries, such as meat-packing, insurance, and electronics.

Manufacturing is changing. Computers are now used to control much factory production. Robots have replaced many workers on the assembly line. Workers in today's modern factories need spe-

out of school to work in the business.

When Hall got to Kansas City, he took a class at a business college to learn how to type. Hall's brothers joined him in the business he started. They began making and selling picture postcards, valentines, and Christmas cards. That was the beginning of Hallmark Cards. Today Hallmark's cards are famous all over the world.

Joyce Hall was an excellent businessman. He closely watched everything that his company did. For many years he approved the drawings for every card the company sold. Joyce Hall thought that it was important to have the very best product. The slogan he chose for Hallmark Cards was "when you care enough to send the very best." For many years Hallmark Cards made the Christmas cards sent by the presidents of the United States.

The boy named Joyce who had been so poor that he had to quit school became one of the richest men in America. He became friends with many famous people including Presidents Harry Truman and Dwight Eisenhower and artist Walt Disney. Joyce Hall and his company also helped Kansas City grow. Hall built the Crown Center development in Kansas City. He also supported many good projects in his city.

cial skills and knowledge to operate the computers and modern equipment.

MINING

Mining has always been important in Missouri. Missouri produces more lead than any other state. As you will remember, the

French found lead in Missouri many years ago. They found the lead near the top of the ground. The miners dug it out with shovels and other hand tools. Today's lead mines are tunnels deep in the earth. Modern machines dig the tunnels and bring the lead out of the ground.

Early Missourians also mined iron. The iron mined in Missouri today is found deep under the ground in southeastern Missouri. Large drills are used to remove it from under the earth. Once it has been brought up, it is made into steel.

Coal is another Missouri mineral. Most Missouri coal is in the Western Plains. Many parts of northern Missouri have coal, but little of it has been mined. There are fewer coal mines operating in Missouri today. Coal was once used to heat homes and businesses. Today coal is used to make electricity.

Missouri's coal is close to the top of the ground. Large machines dig up the thin layer of soil over the coal. The coal is then broken up and taken away. This is known as strip mining. After the coal is taken away, large holes and high mounds of dirt are left behind. The land is often ugly and cannot be farmed. Today, many Missourians are working to make these lands usable again.

Cement is another of Missouri's valuable mineral resources. There are cement plants along the Mississippi and Missouri rivers. The Dundee Cement Company's plant at Clarksville has the world's largest rotary kiln. A kiln is a large furnace used in drying the cement.

FORESTS AND LUMBERING

The trees growing in Missouri are valuable. Early settlers used trees to make their buildings, to build fences, to heat their homes, and to cook their meals.

Today forests are still important. Many trees grow in the Ozark Highland region. Some of the trees are cut down each year. They are made into lumber, fence posts, railroad ties, and charcoal. Hardwood trees are sold for making tool handles, wooden flooring, gunstocks, wooden bowls, and fine furniture.

Missouri forests also provide shelter for wild animals and birds. Deer and turkey are favorite game animals for Missouri hunters. Some forest areas in the Ozarks belong to the United States government. They are part of the Mark Twain National Forest and the Clark National Forest.

RECREATION AND TOURISM

The tourist industry is big business in Missouri today. Millions of people enjoy the state's many different recreational and historic attractions. They hunt, fish, swim, boat, bicycle, hike, and camp in the beautiful Missouri outdoors. Missouri is famous for its fast-

Today the Union Station in St. Louis is the home of a hotel, restaurants, stores, and shops of all kinds.

Missouri Division of Tourism

flowing streams, its beautiful rivers and lakes, and its scenic countryside. The Ozarks is especially popular with tourists. Travelers also visit Missouri's caves and its interesting historic sites and landmarks.

The cities also attract large crowds of tourists looking for fun and recreation. Each year several million fans attend the games of the Kansas City Royals and St. Louis Cardinals baseball teams and the Kansas City Chiefs football team. The St. Louis Art Museum, the History Museum in Forest Park, the St. Louis Symphony, the St. Louis Zoo, and the Muny Opera bring many people to that city. In Kansas City the Nelson-Atkins Art Gallery, the Missouri Repertory Theater, and the Country Club Plaza shopping district also attract visitors from all over the world. So do the Truman Library and the

The Harry S. Truman Library in Independence is a library and museum. The bell on the lawn was given by the people of a small town in France. It is a copy of the American Liberty Bell.

Missouri Division of Tourism

Old Matt's cabin near Branson is a popular tourist attraction in the Ozarks.

Missouri Division of Tourism

National Frontier Trails Center in nearby Independence. Theme parks like Worlds of Fun in Kansas City, Six-Flags over Mid-America in St. Louis, and Silver Dollar City in Branson are also very popular. There are color photographs of several favorite Missouri tourist attractions on pages xii–xiii.

SCHOOLS IN MISSOURI TODAY

The people of Missouri believe everyone should go to school. That is why each year Missouri spends several billion dollars for education. There are laws saying that all young people must attend school.

Schools today are very different from the one-room schools

with only one teacher that many Missouri students attended. The buildings today usually hold many students. They also have several teachers. Schools have more supplies, books, and equipment to make learning easier. Computers have brought many changes to Missouri's classrooms. Today's teachers are much better trained. All teachers today must have a degree from a college or university.

There are many different kinds of schools in the state. Schools teach many things. They teach students how to read, write, and compute. They also teach them history, geography, literature, foreign languages, science, mathematics, computer science, art, music, and dramatic arts.

Missouri's high schools help prepare some students to go to college. They also teach skills to prepare a person for getting a job. Vocational-technical schools help train students for jobs in business, industry, health-care services, farming, and many other fields.

All Missouri schools also provide classes for people with special

Central Missouri State University is one of the state's many fine universities.

Central Missouri State University

needs. The state operates schools for the blind and for the deaf.

Missouri has many good two-year community colleges and four-year colleges and universities. Some of these colleges and universities are public. They receive tax money, but students who attend those schools must also pay some fees to attend. Other colleges and universities are run by churches or other groups.

All schools work to help people live in the age of information services. They also seek to prepare students for living and working with people from other cultures. The modern transportation and communication systems have made it necessary for people from many different parts of the world to work more closely together.

MISSOURIANS ON THE MOVE

Modern Missourians are on the move. Missourians can travel in their motor vehicles along interstate highways and modern hard-surface roads to all parts of the state. Rural residents can drive to a nearby city to shop at a mall or to attend the theater or a ball game. City residents find it easy to drive into the countryside to enjoy the great Missouri outdoors.

The Missouri and Mississippi rivers are still major transportation routes. River barges use these important Missouri waterways to transport grain and other bulky products to many parts of the United States.

Air travel is another important form of transportation in Missouri today. Air travel has changed since Charles Lindbergh flew across the Atlantic Ocean alone in his one-engine plane. Now super-sonic jets can carry several hundred people across that same ocean in only a few hours. People have even walked on the moon.

Missourians have played an important part in these changes. The state has modern airports. Many airlines operate planes that fly in and out of Missouri airports. Missouri factories have produced many airplanes. The Mercury spacecraft was designed and built by a Missouri company. America's first people in space traveled in the Mercury spacecraft.

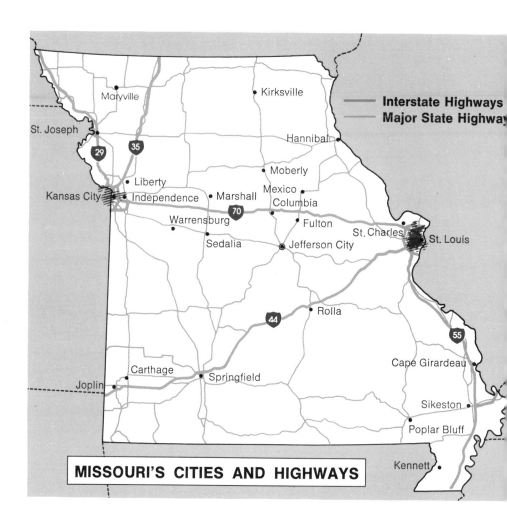

Interstate Highways
Major State Highways

Maryville
Kirksville
St. Joseph
Hannibal
29 35
Moberly
Liberty
Mexico
Kansas City Independence Marshall Columbia
70
Warrensburg
Fulton
Sedalia St. Charles
Jefferson City St. Louis
44 Rolla
55
Carthage
Cape Girardeau
Joplin Springfield
Sikeston
Poplar Bluff
MISSOURI'S CITIES AND HIGHWAYS
Kennett

👉 New Words

manufacture	conservation	tourism
gunstock	tunnel	supersonic
kiln	interstate	erosion

Testing Yourself

1. What are the important products Missouri farmers raise today?

2. Why can farmers today raise more food than pioneer farmers did?

3. What are some of the main products made in Missouri factories today? Are there any factories in your community? If so, what do they make?

4. What are some resources taken from the ground in Missouri?

5. What products are made from trees today?

6. What are some of the special attractions in Missouri that bring tourists into the state?

7. What are some of the different kinds of schools in Missouri?

 # Things to Talk About

1. What kinds of things are computers used for? How have they changed the way we live?

2. What do you think Missouri will be like fifty years from now?

3. Why are schools even more important today than they were in early Missouri?

Books You Can Read

Burchard, S. H. *Sports Star: George Brett*. New York: Harcourt Brace Jovanovich, 1982.

Kansas City: An Intimate Portrait. Kansas City: Hallmark Cards, Inc., 1973.

Lipman, David, and Ed Wilks. *Bob Gibson: Pitching Ace*. New York: Putnam's, 1975.

May, Julian. *The Kansas City Chiefs: Super Bowl Champions*. Mankato, Minn.: Creative Education, 1973.

Neville, Emily Cheney. *Garden of Broken Glass*. New York: Delacorte, 1975. (Fiction)

Robinson, Ray. *Stan Musial: Baseball's Durable "Man."* New York: Putnam's, 1963.

Stolz, Mary. *The Bully of Barkham Street*. New York: Harper, 1985. (Fiction)

————. *A Dog on Barkham Street*. New York: Harper, 1960. (Fiction)

————. *The Explorer of Barkham Street*. New York: Harper, 1985. (Fiction)

Twyman, Gib. *Born to Hit: The George Brett Story*. New York: Random House, 1982.

Chapter 18

FINE ARTS IN MISSOURI

Find the answers to these questions as you read.

What is fiction?

Who were some famous Missouri writers?

Who were some famous Missouri artists?

How did pioneers make music?

What kinds of music came from African-Americans?

Many fine writers, artists, and musicians have come from Missouri. This chapter tells about a few of them.

There are many kinds of writing. There are books, short stories, travel stories, "tall tales," and poems. Some writing is true. In other writing the author makes up the story. It is not about something that really happened. That kind of writing is called fiction. Humorous stories and "tall tales" describe funny people and events. Let's look at some different kinds of writing by Missouri authors.

TRAVEL STORIES

Travelers to Missouri in the early years wrote the first books about the state. Timothy Flint was a traveling minister. He wrote about life in early Missouri and the people he met there. Henry Schoolcraft wrote a book about Missouri lead mines. Henry Brackenridge lived in Ste. Genevieve when he was a boy. He wrote a book about growing up in French Missouri.

Many other travelers also wrote books about Missouri. These books were written long ago. They tell us about life in early Missouri. Travel stories help us today to find out things about Missouri pioneers.

TALL TALES

Other Missouri authors wrote short stories known as "tall tales." They were short funny stories that "stretched the truth." The people in these stories could do almost anything.

Alphonso Wetmore was an early Missouri tall-tale writer. He wrote about a make-believe person called Gall Buster. Gall Buster was stronger than any other person alive. He could escape from dangerous places at the last possible moment. Several short-story writers told about Mike Fink the keelboatman. Mike Fink worked on riverboats on the Mississippi River. Even today these tall tales are fun to read.

SAMUEL L. CLEMENS

The works of Samuel Clemens are very famous. Clemens wrote books and stories. He wrote under the pen name of Mark Twain. Mark Twain is one of America's most important writers. Many of Mark Twain's stories are very funny. But they are more than just amusing. They teach us much about the people around us.

Mark Twain wrote many important books. We cannot name them all here. *The Adventures of Tom Sawyer, Adventures of*

Samuel Clemens is shown here when he was a steamboat pilot.

State Historical Society of Missouri

Huckleberry Finn, *The Prince and the Pauper*, and *Life on the Mississippi* are all famous works. The stories in *Tom Sawyer* and *Huckleberry Finn* take place in Missouri.

OTHER MISSOURI WRITERS

Langston Hughes was a famous Missouri author. He was born in Joplin. He wrote many things, but he is best known as a poet. His writing tells about the lives of blacks in America.

Laura Ingalls Wilder was another popular Missouri writer. She lived on a farm in the Ozarks for many years. In her books, Wilder told about pioneer life. Her exciting stories were written for young people. They tell about Laura and her family when she was a girl. *Little House in the Big Woods*, *Little House on the Prairie*, *Farmer Boy*, *The Long Winter*, and *On the Banks of Plum Creek* are some of her best-known books.

Harold Bell Wright lived in Missouri only a short time, but he wrote books about life in the Ozarks. His most famous book was

FAMOUS MISSOURIANS

Laura Ingalls Wilder Home and Museum

Laura Ingalls Wilder

One summer day three wagons left South Dakota. They were on their way to Missouri. Laura Ingalls Wilder, her husband, her daughter, and a neighbor family had decided to leave South Dakota. For several years it had been too dry the to raise a good crop. There had also been much sickness. The Wilders were going to the Missou Ozarks to live. They had read about "The Land the Big Red Apple." It seemed like it would be good place to live.

The Wilders left South Dakota in July. The tri to Missouri was over six hundred miles. They tr eled across Nebraska and Kansas, camping out along the way. When they finally reached Misso in late August, they liked what they saw. Laura W der thought that the Ozark mountains were beaut ful. The hills were covered with rocks and trees.

The Wilders passed through Springfield. It wa just beginning to become a small city. Laura said that Springfield was the nicest city she had seen The Wilders made their new home in Mansfield was not far from Springfield.

The Shepherd of the Hills. This book was very popular when it was written. It has sold many copies. Every night during the summer a play based on *The Shepherd of the Hills* is performed in Branson near Silver Dollar City.

As Laura Wilder rode in the wagon that summer, she did a lot of thinking. She probably remembered the trips she had made as a young girl. She had been with her parents then. They had moved from their home in the woods in Wisconsin to their house on the prairie in Kansas.

Now, twenty years later, Laura Ingalls Wilder was again making a long trip. This time she was only traveling through Kansas on her way to Missouri. This was the last time she would move. For the rest of her life she lived in Mansfield. The Wilders liked their new home.

Laura Ingalls Wilder loved to read. She had a library in her home in Mansfield. She also liked to write stories. An editor asked her to write something for his magazine. Before long she began writing for many different magazines and newspapers.

Her daughter suggested that she write stories about pioneer life. Her first book was *Little House in the Big Woods*. It told about her life as a young girl in Wisconsin. The book was very popular.

She wrote seven more books. They were printed in twenty-seven different languages. She became very famous for her stories. Her book *Little House on the Prairie* was made into a television series. Today the Wilder home in Mansfield is a museum. Her books are read today more than ever before.

Another well-known writer is Eugene Field. Field was a journalist. His poems for young people are very famous. Two of his most popular poems are "Little Boy Blue" and "Wynken, Blynken, and Nod."

Langston Hughes was a poet. He wrote about African-American life.

State Historical Society of Missouri

Laura Ingalls Wilder lived in this house in Mansfield. She wrote the Little House books there.

State Historical Society of Missouri

Eugene Field was a journalist who also wrote poems for children.

State Capitol mural by Gari Melchers; courtesy State Historical Society of Missouri.

MISSOURI ARTISTS

Many artists and painters have lived in Missouri. George Caleb Bingham, George Catlin, John James Audubon, Thomas Hart Benton, and Walt Disney were particularly famous. Bingham, Catlin, Audubon, and Benton were painters, and Disney was a cartoonist.

George Caleb Bingham lived in Arrow Rock during Missouri's pioneer days. Today you can visit Bingham's home in Arrow Rock. Bingham painted a picture of Daniel Boone moving to Missouri that is very famous. He also painted pictures of everyday life on the frontier. Look again at the color photographs of Bingham's paintings on pages x–xi. Do these scenes tell you something about life in Missouri many years ago?

Two other famous American artists came to Missouri and the West to paint. George Catlin painted many pictures of Indians and Indian life. His drawings are often used in books about Indians. John James Audubon became most famous for his beautiful pictures of birds.

Thomas Hart Benton's mural in the state capitol shows life in Missouri.

Capitol mural by Thomas Hart Benton; courtesy State Historical Society of Missouri

This drawing by Thomas Hart Benton is called *Music Lesson*.

Lithograph by Thomas Hart Benton; courtesy State Historical Society of Missouri

Thomas Hart Benton was another important Missouri artist. He was born in Neosho, but he lived much of his life in Kansas City. Today his home there is a state historic site.

Benton painted many murals. Some of his most famous murals are in Missouri. He painted a mural in the state capitol building in Jefferson City. It shows important things that have happened in Missouri history. One of his murals is in the Truman Library in Independence. It shows the part that city played in helping settle the West.

Walt Disney's name is well known to all Americans. He was a master of make-believe. Disney created Mickey Mouse, Donald Duck, and many other cartoon characters.

Disney was not born in Missouri, but he grew up on a farm near Marceline. Later the family moved to Kansas City. As a boy, Disney liked to draw pictures. Disney went to the Kansas City Art Institute. He liked to draw cartoons, but his cartoons were different. He was not satisfied to see them on paper. He wanted them to move. He made his first moving cartoon films in Kansas City.

From Kansas City, Disney moved to California. There he made his first movie-length cartoons. These cartoons made him world famous. He made movies and television programs. He also started Disneyland.

© Walt Disney Productions

Walt Disney's most famous cartoon characters are Mickey Mouse and Donald Duck.

Scott Joplin wrote many songs that are still enjoyed today.

MUSIC IN MISSOURI

Much of today's music is very different from the music early Missourians enjoyed. Pioneers listened and danced to tunes played by a fiddler. "Buffalo Gals," "Turkey in the Straw," and "Pop, Goes the Weasel" were popular songs.

Missourians also liked ballads. A ballad is a song that tells a story. Many of today's popular songs are also ballads.

Missourians have enjoyed many kinds of music. The German settlers loved music. They started many bands and singing groups. They liked to perform pieces written by famous composers.

African-Americans helped develop special kinds of American music. Blues, ragtime, and jazz are three types of music important to Missouri history. W. C. Handy, Scott Joplin, and William "Count" Basie were all famous African-American composers and musicians. All three spent part of their careers in Missouri.

W. C. Handy is sometimes called the father of the blues. Handy wrote a famous song, "St. Louis Blues." Scott Joplin was the leading writer of ragtime music. He lived in Sedalia. Later he moved to St. Louis. "Maple Leaf Rag" was probably his best-known song. He wrote operas, too. The people of Sedalia hold a music festival to honor this famous American composer.

William "Count" Basie was a famous American jazz musician. He got his start in Kansas City. During the depression, Basie and his band played in many Kansas City nightclubs. Basie moved on to Chicago and New York. Basie made many successful recordings.

Today jazz is popular all over the United States. Each year the Kansas City Jazz Festival and the St. Louis Ragtime Festival are held. They provide great entertainment and remind us that Missourians added much to American music.

Many local communities have musical groups. The St. Louis and Kansas City symphonies are very well known. They play many different kinds of music for their audiences.

New Words

musician	mural	blues
poet	ballad	ragtime
cartoon	composer	fiction
audience		

Testing Yourself

1. What are some different kinds of writing?
2. Who were some of Missouri's most famous writers?
3. Who were some of Missouri's most famous artists?
4. Who were some of Missouri's most famous musicians?
5. What is a pen name?
6. Who created Mickey Mouse and Donald Duck?

Matching Partners

Match the right partners. Write your answers on another sheet of paper.

1. An American writer of ragtime music who began his career in Sedalia

2. An American artist who painted murals in the Missouri State Capitol

3. Wrote under the pen name Mark Twain

4. Painter of everyday frontier scenes who lived at Arrow Rock

5. A poet who wrote about African-Americans

6. Made his first moving cartoons in Kansas City

7. Famous for his paintings of birds

8. Wrote stories about pioneer life

9. A hero in many early tall tales

10. Wrote "St. Louis Blues"

a. Langston Hughes

b. George Caleb Bingham

c. Walt Disney

d. Mike Fink

e. Laura Ingalls Wilder

f. Scott Joplin

g. W. C. Handy

h. Thomas Hart Benton

i. Samuel Clemens

j. John James Audubon

Things to Talk About

1. How are history and fiction different?
2. What kinds of stories do you enjoy reading?
3. Who is your favorite Missouri author? Why?
4. Who is your favorite Missouri artist? Why?

 # Books You Can Read

Anderson, William. *Laura Ingalls Wilder: Pioneer and Author.* New York: Kipling Press, 1987.

Blair, Gwenda. *Laura Ingalls Wilder.* New York: Putnam's, 1981.

Borland, Kathryn K., and Helen R. Speicher. *Eugene Field: Young Poet.* New York: Bobbs-Merrill, 1964.

Daugherty, Charles M. *Samuel Clemens.* New York: Thomas Y. Crowell, 1970.

Dunham, Montrew. *Langston Hughes: Young Black Poet.* New York: Bobbs-Merrill, 1972.

Evans, Mark. *Scott Joplin and the Ragtime Years.* New York: Dodd, Mead, 1976.

Felton, Harold W. *Mike Fink: Best of the Keelboatmen.* New York: Dodd, Mead, 1960.

Field, Eugene. *Poems of Early Childhood.* New York: Charles Scribner's Sons, 1974.

Fisher, Maxine. *The Walt Disney Story.* New York: Franklin Watts, 1988.

Frevert, Patricia D. *Mark Twain: An American Voice.* Mankato, Minn.: Creative Education, 1981.

Graves, Charles P. *Mark Twain.* New York: G. P. Putman's Sons, 1972.

Greene, Carol. *Laura Ingalls Wilder.* Chicago: Childrens Press, 1990.

Hargrove, Jim. *Mark Twain: The Story of Samuel Clemens.* Chicago: Childrens Press, 1984.

Meltzer, Milton. *Langston Hughes: A Biography.* New York: Crowell, 1988.

———. *Mark Twain: A Writer's Life.* New York: Franklin Watts, 1985.

Montgomery, Elizabeth. *Walt Disney: Master of Make-Believe.* Champaign, Ill.: Garrard, 1968.

———. *William C. Handy: Father of the Blues.* Champaign, Ill: Garrard, 1968. (Fictionalized)

Myers, Elisabeth P. *Langston Hughes: Poet of His People.* Champaign, Ill.: Garrard, 1970.

Rollins, Charlemae H. *Black Troubadour: Langston Hughes.* Chicago: Rand McNally and Co., 1970.

Teasdale, Sara. *Stars To-night: Verses New and Old for Boys and Girls.* New York: Macmillan, 1958.

Wilder, Laura Ingalls. *Farmer Boy.* New York: Harper and Row, 1953.

———. *Little House in the Big Woods.* Harper and Row, 1953.

———. *Little House on the Prairie.* New York: Harper and Row, 1953.

Yeo, Wilma, and Helen K. Cook. *Maverick with a Paintbrush: Thomas Hart Benton.* Garden City, N.Y.: Doubleday, 1977.

Appendix

STATE SYMBOLS

A symbol is something that stands for another thing. A flag is a symbol for a country. The American flag is the symbol for the United States. The Gateway Arch has become a symbol for St. Louis. Sports teams use symbols to represent them. The St. Louis Cardinals baseball team uses a redbird as its symbol, and the Kansas City Chiefs football team uses an Indian arrowhead as its symbol. A tiger is the symbol of the sports teams at the University of Missouri in Columbia. Does your school have a symbol? What is it? What other examples of symbols can you give?

States also have symbols to stand for things that are important for that state. Missouri has many important state symbols. You can see a picture of each symbol on pages xiv–xv.

THE MISSOURI STATE SEAL

The Missouri State Seal is the state's official emblem. It contains the Missouri coat of arms. Judge Robert William Wells designed the Great Seal of Missouri. It became the state seal in 1822. There are many symbols in the state seal. The twenty-four stars in the seal show that Missouri was the twenty-fourth state to enter the Union. The two grizzly bears stand for strength and bravery. The state seal also contains the state motto. It is written in Latin. In English it means "the welfare of the people shall be the supreme law." That says that the Missouri government will always try to do what is best for the people of the state. The Roman numerals MDCCCXX stand for 1820, the year that Missouri's first constitution was written.

The Missouri State Seal is impressed on all official papers signed by the governor.

THE MISSOURI STATE FLAG

Missouri has a state flag. Its three stripes are red, white, and blue. They are the same colors as the ones in the United States flag. In the center of the Missouri state flag is a picture of the Missouri coat of arms found in the state seal. The coat of arms is surrounded by a blue band with twenty-four stars.

Missouri did not have a state flag for almost one hundred years after it became a state. Marie Elizabeth Watkins Oliver of Cape Girardeau designed the Missouri state flag. It became the official state flag in 1913. In 1988 elementary students from across Missouri helped raise money to repair the original flag that Mrs. Oliver made. Thanks to their efforts the flag was carefully restored. It is now on display at the Missouri State Archives Building in Jefferson City.

STATE FLOWER

The white hawthorn blossom is the official state flower. The hawthorn is a member of the rose family. It is sometimes called the "red haw" or "white haw." The hawthorn blossoms have greenish-yellow centers and form beautiful white clusters. The hawthorn usually blooms in April and May in Missouri. Many hawthorns can be found in the Ozarks. The hawthorn blossom became the state flower in 1923.

STATE BIRD

The bluebird is the state bird. It has lovely feathers and a soft melodic song. The upper part of its body is covered with light blue feathers, and its breast is a cinnamon red that turns rust-colored in the fall. The bluebird is found throughout Missouri from early spring to late fall. The bluebird is a symbol for happiness. It was made the state bird in 1927.

STATE SONG

"The Missouri Waltz" was once a popular song in Missouri. The General Assembly made it the state song in 1949 when Harry Truman was president. He sometimes played it on his piano.

STATE TREE

The Missouri state tree is the dogwood. The dogwood is a small tree that blooms in the early spring. Its blossoms are lovely white flowers with yellow centers. The General Assembly made it the state tree in 1955.

STATE MINERAL

Galena is the official state mineral. Galena is a shiny, dark gray rock. Lead is made from the galena. Missouri produces more lead than any other state in the United States. Galena was made the state mineral in 1967.

STATE ROCK

Mozarkite is the state rock. It is a beautiful, many-colored rock. Its main colors are green, red, and purple. It can be cut, polished, and used for making jewelry. Mozarkite is found mostly in Benton County. It was made the state rock in 1967.

STATE INSECT

The honeybee is Missouri's state insect. The honeybee is yellow or orange and black. It collects nectar and pollen from flowers in order to produce honey. It is a very valuable insect, but when it is disturbed it sometimes stings people. The honeybee can be found in all parts of the state. It became the state insect in 1985.

STATE MUSICAL INSTRUMENT

Missouri's official musical instrument is the fiddle. Early European settlers and fur traders brought fiddles with them when they came to Missouri. Many different kinds of music can be played on the fiddle. Fiddle music has been popular in Missouri for many years, and good fiddle players can be found in many Missouri communities. The fiddle became the state musical instrument in 1987.

STATE FOSSIL

The crinoid is the official state fossil. A fossil is an impression or trace of a plant or animal preserved in a rock or piece of the earth's crust. The crinoid was once a sea animal that was related to the starfish. It was sometimes called the sea lily because it looked like a plant. It lived in Missouri 250 million years ago. The Missouri General Assembly made the crinoid the state fossil in 1989 because of the efforts of a group of Lee's Summit school students. The students began the project when they were studying about how a law was made in Missouri.

STATE NUT TREE

The state tree is the dogwood, but Missouri also has a state nut tree. It is the black walnut. Walnut trees grow in all parts of the state. Missouri is the leading producer of black walnuts in the United States. The walnut was made the state nut tree in 1990.

MISSOURI DAY

Missouri Day is the third Wednesday in October of each year. It is set apart as a day to remember Missouri history each year. The General Assembly established Missouri Day in 1915.

Acknowledgments

The authors gratefully acknowledge the assistance of the following persons in the preparation of this revised edition:

Katherine Corbett, Mary Seematter, Bryan Thomas, Martha Clevenger, and Jill Wegenstein, Missouri Historical Society, St. Louis.

James W. Goodrich, Fae Sotham, and Mary K. Dains of the State Historical Society of Missouri, Columbia.

Kathryn Carr and Philip Sadler, Central Missouri State University.

Warren Solomon, Missouri Department of Elementary and Secondary Education.

A. Irene Fitzgerald and Adolf E. Schroeder, University of Missouri-Columbia.

Anita Ewing, Trails Regional Library, Warrensburg.

Patricia Woods, The Saint Louis Art Museum.

Senator Harold Caskey, Missouri State Senate.

Betty Gabelsberger, Missouri Division of Tourism.

Dawn Stegeman, Missouri Department of Conservation.

Nick Decker, Missouri Department of Natural Resources.

Cherilyn Williams, Missouri Department of Agriculture.

Chris Fennewald, Missouri Farm Bureau.

Margaret Halliburton, Columbia, Mo.

Glossary

This glossary contains words and names in the book that might be new to you. The meanings of the words have been explained, and the words and names have been respelled to help you say them correctly. The key will show you how to pronounce the different letters. An accent mark (') after a group of letters tells you which letters should be spoken with more force than the others.

Pronunciation Key

a	at, half	ī	ice, sky, high, buy
ay	age, say, aid	ō	oak, toe, open, cork
ah	father, calm	oi	oil, boy
aw	walk, taught, awful	ou	out, owl
e	end, bread, bury	u	flood, up, does
ee	eat, people	ů	full, good, should
ėr	earth, first	oo	threw, food, through, blue
i	build, it, been	uh	alone, complete, circus

abolitionist (ab' uh lish' uhn ist)—a person who worked to free the slaves

acre (ay' kuhr)—a measure of land, 43,560 square feet

ancestor (an' ses tuhr)—a relative or family member who lived long ago

apprentice (uh pren' tis)—a person, usually young, who works for a skilled worker while learning a trade or art

archaeologist (ahr' kee ahl' uh jist)—an expert in archaeology, one who studies the people, customs, and social life of ancient times from the ruins of cities, tools, vessels, and other artifacts

architect (ahr' ki tekt)—a person who draws plans for buildings

artifact (ahr' tu fakt)—a thing or object made by people

assembly line (uh sem' blee līn)—a row of workers or machines along which work is passed until a product is finished

audience (aw' dee unz)—a group of people hearing or seeing something

bale (bayl)—a large bundle of material wrapped for shipping

ballad (bal' uhd)—a simple song or poem that tells a story

barracks (ber' uks)—buildings in which soldiers live

Bequette-Ribault (be kay' ree' bō)—families that built and owned a historic old French house in Ste. Genevieve

Bingham, George Caleb (jōrj' kay' luhb bing' uhm)—a Missouri artist famous for his paintings of frontier life

biography (bī ahg' gruh fee)—the written story of a person's life

bison (bī' suhn)—the buffalo of North America, an animal with a large, shaggy head, strong front legs, and short, thick, curved horns

blacksmith (blak' smith)—a person who makes things from iron

blues (blooz)—songs of sadness performed in a slow, rhythmic way

boatman (bōt' muhn)—a person who uses a boat or works on a boat

bog (bahg)—soft, wet ground

boiler (boi' luhr)—a tank for making steam to heat buildings and to run engines

Bolduc (bōl duk')—a French family that lived in early Ste. Genevieve

bonds (bahndz)—certificates sold promising to pay the owner a certain amount of money with interest at a future date

bookkeeper (bŭk' kee puhr)—a person who keeps a record of money received and spent

border (bōr' duhr)—a line that marks the outer edge or boundary of something

buffalo (buf' uh lō)—see bison

Bruns, Bernhard and Henriette (bern' hahrt and hen ree et' uh broonz)—German immigrants who settled in Missouri

cabinetmaker (kab' uh nit may' kuhr)—a person who builds cabinets, pieces of furniture, or built-in cupboards with shelves

candidate (kan' duh dayt)—a person who seeks or is proposed for an honor or position, often a political office

cannonball (kan' uhn bahl)—a large iron ball fired from a cannon or other heavy gun

canoe (kuh noo')—a small, light boat moved by paddles

capote (kuh pōt')—a long coat or cloak make of rough cloth with a hood

carpenter (kahr' pen tuhr)—a person who builds houses, barns, and other things of wood

cartoon (kahr toon')—an amusing sketch

cavalry (kav' uhl ree)—the branch of an army that fights on horseback or from tanks and other armored vehicles

century (sen' chuhr ee)—a period of 100 years

ceremony (ser' uh mōn ee)—a special form or set of acts to be done on special occasions

chandelier (shand duh lir')—a fixture with several branches of lights, usually hanging from the ceiling

Chouteau, Auguste (ō goost' shoo tō')—a French pioneer settler who helped start St. Louis

clergy (klėr' jee)—people chosen to perform religious duties

climate (klī' muht)—the average weather conditions of a particular place or region, including temperature, rainfall, wind, and sunlight

coastline (kōst' līn)—the outline of the seashore or land along the sea or ocean

colony (kahl' uh nee)—a group of persons who move from their own land to start a settlement somewhere else; the place or country settled by such a group

commander (kuh man' duhr)—a person in charge of an army, ship, or camp; a ruler or leader

commission (kuh mish' uhn)—a group of persons chosen with the authority to do certain things

communist (kahm' yuh nist)—a person who believes in communism, a system in which property is owned by the government rather than by individual persons

composer (kuhm pō' zuhr)—a person who writes music

compromise (kahm' pruh mīz)—a settlement of a dispute in which each side gives up some of its demands

congress (khan' gruhs)—a meeting; a group of people chosen to make laws for a country

conservation (kahn sėr' vay shun)—to keep from wasting or destroying natural resources such as land, timber, water, and minerals

constitution (kahn' stuh too' shun)—the basic law or rules of government for a nation, state, or organized group

consumer (kuhn soo' muhr)—a person who buys or uses a product

continent (kahn' tuh nuhnt)—one of the seven great land masses of the earth

control (kuhn trōl')—to have power over; to hold in check

cooper (koo' puhr)—a person who makes and repairs barrels

copper (kahp' uhr)—a reddish-brown metal that is an excellent carrier of electricity

county (kount' ee)—a division of a state or nation for local government

court (kōrt)—a place where people accused of a crime are brought for trial; the judge or judges and jury appointed to carry out justice

crime (krīm)—an act that is against the law

cupboard (kub' uhrd)—a closet or cabinet with shelves to hold dishes and food items

current (kuhr' uhnt)—the flow of water or air; the flow of electricity

Da Gama, Vasco (vas' kō dah gah' mah)—an early explorer from Portugal who sailed to India

damage (dam' ij)—harm or injury

democracy (di mahk' ruh see)—a government run by the people

depression (di presh' uhn)—a period of time in which business is slow and many people are out of work

descendant (di sen' duhnt)—a family member from a later generation

design (di zīn')—the arrangement of form, detail, and color in a building, a painting, or a weaving; a drawing, plan, or sketch of something to be made

De Soto, Hernando (er nan' dō day sō' to)—an early Spanish explorer who came to North America

Des Peres (de per') **River**—a stream located in south St. Louis

diary (dī' ree)—a daily or weekly written record telling about things that happened

dictator (dik' tayt' uhr)—a ruler who has complete control over a country and its people

diplomat (dip' luh mat)—a person whose job is to conduct official business between his or her country and other countries

Duchesne, Mother Rose Philippine (ruhs' fee lee peen' du shen')—a Catholic nun from France who started schools in early Missouri; a saint in the Catholic Church

Duden, Gottfried (gaht' freed doo' den)—a German lawyer who wrote a book that caused many people to leave Germany and settle in Missouri

dugout (dug' out)—a canoe or boat made by hollowing out a large log

election (i lek' shuhn)—choosing something or someone by voting

electricity (i' lek tris' uh tee)—a form of energy that can produce light, heat, and motion

engineer (en' juh nir')—a person who operates an engine; a person who is skilled in designing buildings, machines, electrical systems, and other things using science and math

equal (eek' wuhl)—the same in size, quality, number, rank, or value

erosion (i rō' shun)—the wearing away of something, such as land, by the action of water or wind

exposition (eks' puh zish' uhn)—a public display or exhibition, such as a world's fair

factory (fak' tuhr ee)—a place where things are made, usually with machines

ferry (fer' ee)—a place were boats carry people and goods across a river or narrow body of water; the boat used in ferrying

fertilizer (fuhr' tuh lī zuhr)—something added to the soil to make it produce more crops

fiction (fik' shun)—a story made up by a writer; something that is not true

flatboat (flat' bōt)—a large boat with a flat bottom and squared ends, often used to float down a river

foreign (fōr' un)—someone or something from another place or country

fortune (fōr' chuhn)—riches or wealth; good luck or success

Fourchet, Jeanette (je net' for shay')—a free black woman who lived and owned property in early St. Louis

fringe (frinj)—a border on a piece of clothing or cloth; something that is on the edge

frontier (frun tir')—the edge of the settled part of a country; a new land or science that offers hope and new benefits

furnace (fuhr' nis)—a closed chamber where heat is produced, such as heating for a house

furs (fuhrz)—the soft hair covering the skins of certain animals

gallop (gal' uhp)—to run with a series of springs and leaps, as a galloping horse

game (gaym)—a contest played according to set rules; wild animals, birds, and fish hunted or caught for food and sport

general assembly (jen' uhr uhl a sem' blee)—a group of people elected to make laws for a state

Genoa (jen' ō uh)—a city in Italy

government (guv' uhrn muhnt)—rule over a country, state, district; the system of ruling

governor (guv' uhr nuhr)—a person selected to be in charge of something; the main leader of a state

guerrillas (guh rill' uhz)—bands of armed fighters who are not a part of the regular army

gumbo (gum' bō)—a soup thickened with okra pods

gunstock (gun' stahk)—the wooden handle to which the barrel of a gun is fastened

harsh (hahrsh)—coarse or rough to the touch; severe, unfeeling

hatred (hay' trid)—a very strong dislike, ill will

heirloom (er' loom)—a family possession handed down from generation to generation

hemp (hemp)—a plant used to make rope, heavy string, and coarse cloth

hominy (haw' mi nee)—a food made from hulled corn

immigrant (i' mi gruhnt)—someone who leaves one country and settles in another one

income tax (in' kuhm taks)—a tax on money earned by people or companies

independence (in' dee pen' dens)—freedom from control, support, or help of others

infection (in fek' shuhn)—a causing of disease in people, animals, or plants by germs

interstate (in' tuhr stayt')—between states

invent (in vent')—to make up or to produce for the first time

Iraq (i rahk')—a country in the Middle East

island (ī' luhnd)—an area of land that is smaller than a continent and completely surrounded by water

jayhawker (jay' hah' kuhr)—the name given to people from Kansas who attacked settlements in Missouri at the time of the Civil War; someone from Kansas

jazz (jaz)—music marked by lively rhythms in which accented notes fall at unusual places

Jolliet, Louis (loo ee' jō lee ay')—an early French trader and explorer who came to Missouri

judge (juj)—a government official having the power to preside over and to answer certain questions brought before a court

jury (joo' ree)—a group of persons selected to hear evidence in a law court and give a decision on that evidence

kerosene (ker' uh seen)—a thin oil sometimes used for burning in a cooking stove, lamp, or heater

kettle (ket' uhl)—a pot used for boiling liquids

kiln (kiln)—an oven or furnace used for heating things to give them a proper finish

kindergarten (kin' duhr gahr tuhn)—a school or class for children from about four to six years of age

Korea (kō ree' uh)—a country in Asia

Laclede, Pierre (pee er' la kled')—a French trader who helped start St. Louis

La Guignolee (la gin yō lay')—an old French song sung on New Year's Eve by people going from house to house

lard (lahrd)—fat from hogs used for cooking

La Salle, Sieur de (Robert Cavelier) (rō ber' ka vel yay' soor' duh la sal')—an early French explorer in North America

lawyer (law' yuhr)—a person whose work is giving advice to others about the laws or acting for others in court

license (lī' suhnz)—a permit from a government allowing someone to do a certain thing

licorice (lik' uhr ish)—a black, sweet-tasting, gummy extract from a plant; candy flavored with this extract

limp (limp)—to walk lamely or uneasily

Lindbergh, Charles (charls lin' buhrg)—the first pilot to fly a plane alone across the Atlantic Ocean

livestock (līv' stahk)—farm animals, such as cows, horses, sheep, or hogs

loft (lawft)—a space just below the roof of a building

loom (loom)—a frame or machine used for weaving cloth

Louis XIV (loo ee' the fourteenth)—a French king

machine (muh sheen')—a device with moving parts that performs a task in repairing or making something

magazine (mag' uh zeen)—a publication appearing at regular times with stories and articles by various writers

mammoth (mam' uhth)—a huge, hairy, elephant-like animal with long curved tusks that no longer exists

mansion (man' shuhn)—a large, fine house

manufacture (man yuh fak' chuhr)—the making of products by hand or by machine

Marquette, Father Jacques (jahk' mahr ket')—an early French missionary and explorer who came to Missouri

mastodon (mas' tuh dahn)—a very large animal like an elephant that no longer lives on the earth

mayor (may' uhr)—a person chosen to be the main leader of a city or town

medical (med' uh kuhl)—having to do with medicine or the treatment of disease or injury

merchant (mėr' chuhnt)—a storekeeper, a person who buys and sells things

mineral resource (min' uhr uhl ree' sōrs)—material having value that is taken from the earth

missionary (mish' uh ner ee)—a person going out to do religious work

moccasin (mahk' uh suhn)—a soft leather shoe or sandal without a heel

Mo'n Sho'n A-ki-Da Tonkah (mahn' shahn' ah kee dah tahn' kuh)—Big Soldier's Indian name

mortar and pestle (mōr' tuhr and pes' uhl)—a container (mortar) and a club-shaped tool (pestle) used for grinding or pounding something into a powder

mule (myool)—an animal that is the offspring of a donkey and a horse

mural (myu' ruhl)—a picture, usually of great size, painted on a wall

museum (myoo zee' uhm)—a building where objects of interest are displayed and kept

musician (myoo zish' uhn)—a person who writes, sings, or plays music skillfully

newcomer (noo' cu muhr)—a person who has just come to a place

nuclear (nyoo' klee uhr)—something using atomic energy or power

nun (nun)—a woman who devotes her life to religion and who lives under religious vows or promises she has made

officer (ahf' i suhr)—someone with a special job in a business, an organization, or the government; a person in charge of others in the military service

Osage (ō' sayj)—an Indian tribe that lived in Missouri

parka (pahr' kuh)—a hooded jacket worn in cold weather

peace (pees)—the absence of war; quiet; stillness

pelisse (puh lees')—a long, loose-fitting coat

perfumes (puhr' fyoomz)—liquids with the sweet smell of flowers

plains (playnz)—broad stretches of flat land

plantation (plan tay' shuhn)—a large farm on which cotton, tobacco, sugarcane, coffee, or other crops are raised and worked by laborers who live there

plaster (plas' tuhr)—a soft, sticky mixture that hardens when it dries and is used for walls and ceilings

plaza (pla zuh)—a public square in a city or town

plow (plou)—a farm tool that is usually pulled and that cuts and turns over the soil

poet (pō' uht)—a person who writes poems, which are words in verse that convey to the reader special ideas or thoughts

politician (pahl uh tish' uhn)—a person who takes an active part in running the government

portrait (pōr' trayt)—a picture of a person showing his or her face

power (pou' uhr)—strength; the ability to act or do, control over

prehistoric (pree his tōr' ik)—having to do with the time before people began writing down what happened in their lives

product (prahd' uhkt)—anything that is grown, made, or manufactured

professional (pruh fesh' uh nuhl)—one whose occupation requires special education and training, such as a teacher, a lawyer, or a doctor; one who makes a business or trade of something others do for fun, as a professional baseball player

profit (prah' fit)—to make money from a business; the money made from a business

property (prah' puhr tee)—something that is owned, a possession

property tax (prah' puhr tee taks)—a tax on property

quilt (kwilt)—a bed covering made of two layers of material with a filling of wool, cotton, or feathers

ragtime (rag' tīm)—music with the accents or strong beats coming at unusual places

rank (rangk)—position, grade, or official standing in the army; a certain place in a special order or list

reaper (ree' puhr)—a machine for harvesting grain

Reconstruction (ree' kuhn struk' shuhn)—the period of time after the Civil War when the Southern states were reorganized

recycle (ree sī' kulh)—to process something so that it can be used again

Renault, Philippe (fee leep' re nō')—an early French lead miner who came to Missouri

retreat (ree treet')—to withdraw from danger, to move back

rifle (rī' fuhl)—a gun having a long barrel, usually shot from one's shoulder

rights (rītz)—things to which a person has a legal claim

robot (rō' baht)—a machine that does jobs usually done by people

Sac (sahk)—an Indian tribe

Sacajawea (sahk' a jah wee' uh)—an Indian woman who traveled with the Lewis and Clark expedition

sales tax (saylz taks)—a tax paid on things that you buy

sandbar (sand' bahr)—a ridge of sand in a river

sauerbraten (sour' braht un)—roast beef soaked in vinegar and spices before cooking

sauerkraut (sour' krout)—finely cut cabbage salted and soured in its own juice

segregate (seg' ruh gayt)—to separate from others, set apart, isolate

senator (sen' uh tuhr)—a member of the senate, which is a body of citizens with the power to make laws

Shawnee (shaw nee')—an Indian tribe

shingles (shing' guhlz)—pieces of wood or other material that are used to cover roofs, walls, and so forth

shutters (shut' uhrz)—movable covers for a window, usually a pair

slaughter (slaw' tuhr)—the killing of animals for food; butchering

snag (snag)—a tree stump or branch stuck in a river that can damage a boat

soybeans (soi' beenz)—a plant grown for animal food, vegetable oil, flour, and meal

spring (spring)—to leap; to jump up; a flow of water coming from the earth; a season of the year

stables (stay' buhlz)—buildings in which horses or cattle are kept

stagecoach (stayj' kōch)—a horse-drawn, four-wheeled carriage used for passengers and mail

steamboat (steem' bōt)—a boat, especially a riverboat, moved by a steam engine

submarine (sub' muh reen)—a boat that can operate underwater

succotash (suk' uh tash)—a food of beans and corn cooked together

supersonic (soo puhr sahn' ik)—faster than the speed of sound

supplies (suh plīz')—things like food, clothing, and guns that are needed by an army, expedition, or other group

swampland (swahmp' land)—low-lying land that collects water and is always wet and spongy

tariff (ter' uhf)—a system of taxes that a government charges on things brought into a country

taxes (tak' siz)—money taken from citizens to pay for the cost of government and public services

temperate (tem' puhr uht)—a climate that is not very hot or very cold

theater (thee' uh tuhr)—a place or building where plays, movies, and other programs are presented to an audience

tobacco (tuh bak' ō)—a product that is smoked or chewed and is made from the dried leaves of the tobacco plant

tourism (tur' is uhm)—travel for fun and recreation

treaty (tree' tee)—an official agreement between nations

troops (troopz)—soldiers; a group or band of people

tunnel (tun' uhl)—an underground passageway

turbine (tur' buhn)—an engine or motor that is run by the force of water, steam, or air

uniform (yoo' nuh form)—clothes of a particular style worn by persons in the same service or order, as soldiers or policemen; the same

upstream (up' streem)—toward the source or beginning of a river or stream; against the current of a river

Valle, Francois II (fran swah' val lay' the second)—a French merchant and leader in early Ste. Genevieve

victory (vik' tuhr ee)—the defeat of an enemy in combat or war; success in a contest

Vietnam (vee et nahm')—a country in Asia

vote (vōt)—to express one's wish or choice in a formal way

warehouse (wer' hous)—a building where goods are kept; storehouse

warp (wohrp)—to bend out of shape

whitewash (hwīt' wahsh)—a mixture of lime and water painted on walls or fences to whiten them

Yankee (yang' kee)—a person from the northern part of the United States

Index

Abolitionists, 155
Adair County, 217
Africa, 21, 37, 62
African-Americans, 81, 142
    brought from Africa, 149
    in French Missouri, 57
    and slavery, 45, 52, 57, 62, 149–52
    and freedom, 56, 57, 152–55, 156,
        180–81
    during the Civil War, 164
    after the Civil War, 179–84
    and segregation, 219, 220–21, 235–
        38
    in Civil Rights movement, 219, 235–
        38
Agriculture. See Farming
Alabama, 161, 184
Allies (in World War I), 208
Allies (in World War II), 226, 231
Altenberg, 135
American Association of University
    Women, 238
American Missionary Association, 182
American Revolutionary War, 70–71
American Royal Livestock and Horse
    Show, 199
Anderson, Bill, 169, 170
Anderson House (Lexington), 167
Anheuser-Busch, 257
Antarctica, 21
Archaeologists, 1–2, 4–5
Arctic Ocean, 22
Arkansas, 23, 161, 167, 172
Arnold, 27
Arrow Rock, x, 121, 140–41, 142, 275
Arrow Rock Tavern, 119, 121
Artists, 140–41, 275–77
Ashley, William H., 119
Asia, 21, 36, 231
Atlantic Ocean, 22, 53, 71
Audubon, John James, 275

Austria-Hungary, 208
Aull, James, 139
Austin, Moses, 124
Austin, Stephen, 60, 124
Austin (Texas), 124
Australia, 21
Automobiles, 188, 193–95, 213–14
Axis Powers (World War II), 226, 231

Bagnell Dam, 30
Ballwin, 25
Baptists, 98, 155
Basie, William "Count," 221, 279
Bass, Tom, 199
Becknell, William, 120
Beckwourth, James P., 119, 120–21
Bell, Alexander Graham, 187
Belton, 25
Benton, Thomas Hart (artist), 143, 275,
    277
    paintings and drawings by, 276
Benton, Thomas Hart (U.S. senator), 143–
    44, 157, 163
Bequette-Ribault House, 54, 57
Bering Sea, 3
Berkely, 25
Bicycles, 194, 195
Big Soldier (Osage leader), 14–15
Big Spring, 26, 27
Bill of rights, 83, 248
Bingham, George Caleb, 140–41, 275
    home (Arrow Rock), x
    paintings by, x, xii, 143
Bingham, Mary, 140
Birthright, Bettie and Charles, 183, 184
Bison, prehistoric, 4
Black Robes, 40
Blacks. See African-Americans
Blair, Emily Newell, 215
Blair, Francis P., Jr. (Frank), 162–63,
    178

Blow, Susan Elizabeth, 196–97
Bluebird, xiv, 284
Blue Springs, 25
Bluford, Lucille, 219, 236–37
Bolduc House, 54–55, 57
Bolivar, 126
Boone, Daniel, 71–73, 141, 275
Boone, Daniel Morgan, 71–72
Boone, Nathan, 73
Boone, Rebecca, 71–73
Boonville, 81, 93, 168, 181
Booth, John Wilkes, 177
Border ruffians, 156
Brackenridge, Henry, 60, 270
Bradley, Omar, 226, 227
Branson, 263, 272
Bridger, Jim, 119
Bridgeton, 25
Briggs, Mrs. C. A., 182
Brighton, 126
Brown, William Wells, 152–56
Bruce, Blanche, 183
Bruns, Henriette and Bernhard, 136–37
Buffalo, 4, 8
Bulgaria, 208
Bushwhackers, 169, 172
Business and Professional Women's Association, 238
Butterfield, John, 126
Butterfield Overland Mail Company, 126

Cahokia (Illinois), 6
California, 121, 125, 126, 127–28, 277
California Trail, 123
Camp Crowder, 228
Camp meetings, 95–96, 98
Canada, 22, 40, 42, 69, 154
Cape Girardeau, 27, 58, 209, 284
Capital cities, of Missouri, 84–85
Capitol buildings, Missouri, xvi, 84–85
Caribbean Sea, 40, 234
Carrollton, 256
Carson, Christopher "Kit," 119, 122–23
Carthage, 27
Cassville, 126
Catholic Church, 40, 65, 96–97
Catlin, George, 275
Central America, 40, 234
Central Missouri State University, 264
Central Powers (World War I), 208

Cherokee Indians, 181
Chesterfield, 25
China, 38
Chouteau, Auguste, 46–47, 57, 62
Chouteau, Marie Therese, 47
Chouteau, Pierre, 62
Chouteau, Pierre, Jr., 119
Christman, Paul, 221
Churches
    African-American, 155, 183
    Baptist, 98, 155
    Catholic, 40, 65, 96–97
    Presbyterian, 184
Cincinnati (Ohio), 154
Circuit riders, 95
Civilian Conservation Corps, 218
Civil rights movement, 219, 235–38
Civil War
    causes of, 157–58
    in Missouri, 162–63, 165–72
    results of, 172, 176
Clark, William, 76–77, 79, 117, 124
Clark National Forest, 261
Clarksville, 260
Clarkton, 184
Clayton, 25
Clemens, Samuel (Mark Twain), 108–9, 270–71
Clever, 126
Climate, types of, 30–32
Cockrell, Francis Marion, 178
Coff, Edward, 189–90
Cole family, 92–94
Columbia, 25, 141, 214, 258
Columbus, Christopher, 37–39
Communication
    by Pony Express, 127–28
    by radio, 214
    by telegraph, 128
    by telephone, 187, 195
Confederate States of America, 157–58, 161, 163
Constitutions, of Missouri, 83–84, 247–48
Continents, 21
Counties, 250–51
Country Club Plaza (Kansas City), 262
Courts, Missouri, 249
Creve Coeur, 25, 200
Crinoid, xv, 286
Crow Indians, 121

Crown Center (Kansas City), 259
Cuba, 40, 211
Current River, xii, 26

Da Gama, Vasco, 37
Davis, Jefferson, 158
Declaration of Independence, 70, 99
Defiance, 73
Deere, John, 138–39
Delaware Indians, 13, 101
Democracy, 244
Depression, Great, 207, 216–17
De Soto, Hernando, 39
Des Peres River, French settlement at,
    44
Disney, Walt, 275, 277
Dogwood, xiv, 285
Duchesne, Rose Philippine, 96–97
Duden, Gottfried, 135
Dundee Cement Company, 260

Eads, James, 192
Eads Bridge, 192–93
Eastern Hemisphere, 22
East Indies, 38
Eastman, George, 188
Easton, Rufus, 82
Edison, Thomas, 187
Elkton, 126
England, 40, 69
    settlers from, 53
    and American Revolution, 70–71
Europe, 7, 21, 69, 73, 134, 141, 155,
    208–11
Europeans
    and a shorter route to Asia, 36–37
    and the Indians, 7–9
Equator, 21

Factories, 142, 195–98, 257
Farming
    by Native Americans, 5, 7, 10–11
    by French, 45, 61, 63
    in the 1800s, 89–92, 138–39, 148,
        199
    during World War I, 211
    during World War II, 227
    today, 25–27, 255–56
Farmland Industries, 256
Ferguson, 25
Fiddle, xv, 286

Field, Eugene, 273, 275
Fink, Mike, 270
Flatboats, 105–7
Flint, Timothy, 270
Florida (state), 161
Florida (town), 108
Florissant, 25, 97
Food
    African-American, 63
    French, 62–63
    on the frontier, 91–92, 101
    Native American, 5, 10–11, 13, 60, 63
Ford, Henry, 213
Forests and lumbering, 26, 260–61
Fort Davidson, 168
Fort Leonard Wood, 228, 229
Fort Orleans, 44
Fort Osage, 80, 82–83
Fort Sumter (South Carolina), 158
Fourchet, Jeanette, 56, 156
Fox Indians, ix, 13
Fox Theatre, 214
France, 40, 69–70, 71, 73, 74, 208, 226
Franklin, 81, 121, 123, 140
French
    cooking, 62–63
    explorers in America, 40
    farming, 52, 53, 61, 63
    fur traders, 52, 61–62
    houses, 53–54
    and the Indians, 58–60
    lead mining, 43–44, 52, 62
    missionaries, 40–43, 44, 52
    settlers in Missouri, 43–44, 52, 53
    way of life, 52–57
    women, ix, 62
Frontier
    books, 100
    churches, 95–96
    farming, 91–92
    food, 91–92, 101
    fun, 97–100
    homes, 90–91
    Ozarks, 100–101
Fulton, 25
Fur trade
    French, 48, 61–62
    American, 117–20

Gaines, Lloyd, 219
Galena, xv, 285

Gasconade River, 101, 107
Gateway Arch (St. Louis), xiii, 117, 283
General Assembly, Missouri, 248–49
Geographic regions, of Missouri, 24–27
Georgia, 161
Germans, 135–38, 163
Germany, 208, 225–26
Gladstone, 25
Glasgow, 107
Government
    in the 1800s, 142–43, 178
    of cities, 250–51
    of counties, 251
    kinds of, 244–49
    of Missouri, 247–48
    reasons for, 243–44
    taxes and, 251
    of the United States, 244–46
Governor, of Missouri, 249
Graham Cave, 4–5
Grandview, 25, 232
Grant, Ulysses S., 181
Great Britain, 208
Great Lakes, 40, 154
Great Plains, 127
Grenada, 234
"Guignolee, La," 65
Gulf of Mexico, 22, 42

Hall, Joyce C., 258–59
Hallmark Card Company, 258–59
Handy, W. C., 278–79
Hannah's Fort, 93
Hannibal, 25, 107, 108–9, 195
Hannibal Bridge (Kansas City), 192
Hannibal & St. Joseph Railroad, 112
Harris, William Torrey, 196
Hawthorn, xiv, 284
Hazelwood, 25
Hermann, 93, 135
History Museum (Forest Park, St. Louis),
    216, 262
Hitler, Adolf, 226
Honeybee, xv, 285
Hopewell people, 5
House of Representatives, Missouri, 249
Houses
    American, 79
    French, 45, 53–55, 57
    frontier log cabins, 90–91
    Osage, 11–12
Hughes, Langston, 271, 274

Illinois, 23, 155, 181
Independence, 25, 121, 122, 139, 156,
    209, 231, 233, 263
India, 38
Indians. See Native Americans
Iowa, 22
Ioway Indians, 13
Ireland, 138
Irish, 137–38
Isabella, Queen of Spain, 38
Italy, 225–26

Jacks Fork River, 101
Jackson, Andrew, 143, 162
Jackson, Claiborne, 162, 164, 165
Jackson County, 80, 209, 232
James, Frank, 170
James, Jesse, 170
James River, 101
Japan, 225–26, 231
Jayhawkers, 157
Jefferson, Thomas, 15, 70, 76–77, 79, 85
Jefferson Barracks, 228
Jefferson City, xvi, 27, 85, 107, 136, 137,
    143, 164, 168, 181, 214, 277, 284
Jefferson County, 194
Johnson, Andrew, 177
Jennings, 25
Jolliet, Louis, 40–42
Joplin, Scott, 278, 279
Joplin (town), 26, 191, 198, 271

Kansas, 23, 156–57, 272, 273
Kansas City, 13, 25, 277, 279
    in the 1800s, 138, 139, 141, 142, 168
    in the 1900s, 191, 195, 197–98, 214,
        221, 258–59
    today, 258, 262–63
Kansas City Call, 237
Kansas City Chiefs, 262, 283
Kansas City Jazz Festival, 279
Kansas City Monarchs, 226–27
Kansas City Royals, 262
Kansas City Symphony, 279
Kansas Indians, 13
Keelboats, 106–7
Kelly, Margaret, 238
Kennett, 27
Kentucky, 23, 71, 81, 152, 154, 162
Keytesville, 234
Kickapoo Indians, 13, 101
Kindergartens, 196–97

Kirksville, 25, 219
Kirkwood, 25
Knob Noster, 226
Korea, 231, 234
Kuwait, 235

Labor Unions, 197
Laclede, Pierre, 46, 48
Laclede (town), 210
Ladue, 25
Lafayette County Courthouse, 168
Lamar, 209, 232, 233
La Salle, Robert Cavelier, sieur de, 42
Lead. See Mining
League of Women Voters, 215, 238
Lee's Summit, 25
Lewis, Meriwether, 76–77, 79, 117, 124
Lexington, 107, 127, 139, 167, 168, 171,
    172
Lexington, battle of, 167
Liberia, 181
Liberty, 25, 139
Liberty Memorial (Kansas City), 212
Libraries, 47, 100
Lincoln, Abraham, 157–58, 162, 177
Lincoln, Tad, 158
Lincoln University, 181, 182, 219
Lindbergh, Charles A., 215–16, 265
Lindenwood Colleges, 83
Literature, 269–74
Lone Star Republic, 124
Lorimier, Louis, 58
Louis XIV (King of France), 42
Louisiana (state), 161
Louisiana (territory), 42, 69–70, 73–75,
    83
Louisiana Purchase, 73–75, 85
Louisiana Purchase Exposition, 188–91
Lyon, Nathaniel, 163, 166

McCormick, Cyrus, 139
McDonnell Douglas Corporation, 257
McNair, Alexander, 84
Maine, 82
Majors, Alexander, 127
Mammoth, 3–4
Mansfield, 272, 273
Maplewood, 25
Marceline, 277
Mark Twain National Forest, 261
Marquette, Father Jacques, 40–42
Marshall, 25

Marthasville, 152
Maryland Heights, 25
Maryville, 25
Mastodon, 3–4
Mays family, 218–19
Meachum, John Berry, 154–55, 156, 180
"Meet Me in Saint Louie," 191
Memphis (Tennessee), 40
Mendenhall, Willard and Mollie, 171–72
Meramec River, 14
Mexicans, 116
Mexico (country), 22, 39, 40, 124, 211
Mexico (town), 25, 199
Miami, 13
Mid-America Dairymen, 256
Midland Theater, 214
Mining
    in the 1900s, 25, 26
    of coal, 191, 260
    of iron, 260
    of lead, 43, 61–62, 191, 260
    of zinc, 191
    today, 259–60
Minor, Virginia, 185
Mississippi (state), 161, 183
Mississippi people, 6–7
Mississippi River, 14, 27–29, 40–42,
    44, 45, 48, 61, 71, 74, 81, 85, 111,
    270
Missouri, origin of name, 14–15
Missouri Commission on Human Rights,
    237
Missouri Compromise, 83
Missouri Day, 286
Missouri Equal Rights League, 181
Missouri Farm Bureau, 256
Missouri Farmers Association (MFA), 256
Missouri Indians, 12, 46
Missouri National Guard, 209
Missouri Repertory Theater (Kansas
    City), 262
Missouri River, 14, 27–29, 41–42, 44, 48,
    61, 81, 85, 93, 117, 118
Missouri State Highway Patrol, 214
Missouri Territory, 77, 81
"Missouri Waltz," 285
Moberly, 25
Monsanto Company, 257
Montgomery County, 4
Motion pictures, 214, 220
Mountain men, 118–19
Mozarkite, xv, 285

Mules, 121–22
Museum of Westward Expansion
   (St. Louis), 117
Music, 278–79

Napoleon Bonaparte, 73
National Association for the Advancement of Colored People (NAACP),
   237
National Farmers Organization, 256
National Frontier Trails Center (Independence), 121, 263
National Organization for Women
   (NOW), 238
Native Americans
   and the American frontier, 71, 92, 93,
     116–18, 120, 275
   contributions of, 13–14
   before the Europeans came, 1, 3–7
   after the Europeans came, 7–9
   and farming, 5, 7, 10–11
   and the French, 58–60
   as traders, 7–8, 44, 58–59
   words of, 13, 14–15
   See also names of individual tribes
Nebraska, 23, 272
Nelson-Atkins Art Galley (Kansas City),
   262
Neosho, 13, 228
New Madrid, 27
New Mexico, 119
New Orleans, 44, 48, 73–74, 153
New York, 108
Niangua River, 14
Nichols Fountain (Kansas City), xiii
Niña (ship), 38
North America, 21, 23, 39, 40, 73
North Carolina, 81, 161
Northern Hemisphere, 21–22
Northern states, 82, 134, 147–49, 157–
   58

Ohio, 153, 180
Oklahoma, 23, 181
Oliver, Marie Elizabeth Watkins, 284
Order No. Eleven, xi, 141
Oregon, 124–25
Oregon Trail, 123, 124
Orient, 36
Osage County, 136

Osage Indians, 7, 9–12, 14, 46
Osage River, 14, 30, 107
Osceola, 13
Ozarks, xii, 26–27, 43, 110–11, 191,
   271, 272
Ozarks, Lake of the, xii, 30

Pacific Ocean, 22
Pacific Railroad, 112
Paige, Satchel, 221
Panama, 234
Parks, in Missouri, 214
Pea Ridge, battle of, 170
Pearl Harbor, 226
Peoria Indians, 13, 58
Perry, Ivory, 237–38
Pershing, John J., 209–11
Persian Gulf, 234–35
Peters, Nellie, 214
Phelps, Mary Whitney, 170
Philadelphia (Pennsylvania), 108–9, 141
Philippine Islands, 211
Piankashaw Indians, 101
Pilot Knob, 168
Pinta (ship), 38
Plank roads, 111–12
Poland, 226
Pomme de Terre, Lake, 30
Pony Express, 127–28
Poplar Bluff, 27
Portugal, 36
Potosi, 60
Presbyterian Church, 184
Price, Sterling, 165, 166, 168, 171
Prime Meridian, 22
Protest movements, 238
Pruitt, Wendell, 227
Pulaski County, 228, 229

Quantrill, William C., 170

Radicals, in Reconstruction, 177, 178–
   79
Radio, 214
Railroads, 112, 191–93
Ralston Purina, 257
Randolph County, 226
Raytown, 25
Reconstruction
   African-Americans during, 179–83

business during, 176–77, 178
   government during, 178
Revels, Hiram, 183
Richmond, 139
Religion
   and the French, 65
   on the frontier, 95–96
Renault, Philippe, 62
Richmond Heights, 25
Roads, 104–5, 111
Roaring Twenties, 207, 212–14
Rocky Mountains, 117, 120–21, 127
Rolla, 27
Roosevelt, Franklin D., 231, 233
Russell, Majors and Wadell, 127
Russell, William B., 127
Russia, 208, 211, 226

Sacajawea, 77, 78
Sac Indians, ix, 13
St. Ann, 25
St. Charles, xvi, 25, 79, 83, 85, 96–97
Ste. Genevieve, 43, 44–45, 57, 58, 60,
   62, 65–66, 270
St. Joseph, 25, 107, 124, 127, 128, 138,
   191, 258
St. Louis
   founding of, 48
   before the Louisiana Purchase, 6–7,
      25, 46, 47, 48, 57, 61, 71
   in the 1800s, 79, 107, 112, 118, 134,
      138, 152, 153, 154–55, 162, 163,
      168, 180, 181, 183, 185, 196–97
   in the 1900s, 188, 191, 195, 197, 214,
      216, 221
   today 257, 262–63
St. Louis Art Museum, 262
St. Louis Browns, 202
St. Louis Cardinals, 202, 262, 283
St. Louis Ragtime Festival, 279
St. Louis Symphony, 262, 279
St. Louis World's Fair. See Louisiana Pur-
   chase Exposition
St. Louis Zoo, 262
St. Peters, 25
Saline County, 5, 9, 12
Salt making, 43–44
Saluda (steamboat), 111
Santa Fe trade, 119–22
Santa Fe Trail, 123

Santa Maria (ship), 38
Santo Domingo, 40
Schoolcraft, Henry, 270
Schools
   for African-Americans, 155, 180, 181,
      182
   before the Civil War, 94–95, 96–97
   after the Civil War, 178–79, 196–97
   French, 64
   today, 263–65
Scott, Harriet and Dred, 152
Sedalia, 25, 112, 191, 279
Sedalia Army Air Field, 231
Segregation, 183, 235–38
Senate, Missouri, 249
Shawnee Indians, 13, 59, 101
Shiloh, Battle of, 181
Sibley, Mary Easton and George C.,
   82–83
Sikeston, 27
Silver Dollar City (Branson), 263
Six Flags over Mid-America (St. Louis),
   263
Slaves, 81, 134, 148
   before the Civil War, 157
   freeing of, 178, 179
   French, 45, 52, 57, 62, 65
   lives of, 149–52
   and statehood, 82, 84
Smith, Jedediah, 119
South America, 21, 39, 40, 126
South Carolina, 81, 157, 161
South Dakota, 272
Southern Hemisphere, 22
Southern states, 82, 134, 147–49, 157–
   58
Southwestern Bell, 257
Spain, 38, 40, 41–42, 69–70, 71
Spanish
   explorers, 39–40
   settlers, 116
Spirit of St. Louis, 215, 216
Sports, 202, 220–21
Springfield, 26, 126, 166, 191, 198, 258,
   272
Stagecoaches, 126–27
Steamboats, 107–11
Stoddard, Amos, 75
Stores, 199–202
Sullivan, Leonor Kretzer, 238

Symbols, of Missouri, xiv-xv, 283–86
Symington, Stuart, 246–47

Table Rock Lake, 30
Tariff, 148
Taum Sauk Mountain, 27
Taylor, Maxwell, 234
Telegraph, 128
Telephone, 187, 195
Tennessee, 23, 81, 161
Texas, 124, 161
Tipton, 126
Tourism, 261–63
Transportation
    by aircraft, 215–16, 265
    by flatboat, 74, 105–7
    by French cart, 60
    by keelboat, 106–7
    by railroad, 112, 191–93
    by river, 79, 104–11
    on early roads, 104–5
    by steamboat, 107–11
    today, 265
    by wagon and stagecoach, 126–27
Truman, Harry S., 208–9, 230, 231, 232, 233
Truman Lake, 30
Truman Library, 233, 262, 277
Turkey, 208
Turner, James Milton, 180–81, 182
Turner, John, 180
Twain, Mark. See Samuel Clemens

U-boats (submarines), 208
Union Station (St. Louis), 261
United Nations, 233
United States Congress, 81, 82, 83, 84, 236, 245
United States Military Academy (West Point), 58, 161, 210
United States Supreme Court, 236, 237, 245
University City, 25
University of Missouri–Columbia, 141, 199, 202, 203, 219, 236, 255, 283
USS Missouri, 230, 231, 235

Valle family, 65–66
Van Meter State Park, 5

Vespucci, Amerigo, 39
Vietnam, 231, 234
Virginia, 81, 140, 154, 161

Waddell, W. B., 127
Wappapello, Lake, 30
Warrensburg, 25, 182
Warsaw, 126
Washington, George, 71, 211
Washington, D.C., 15, 177, 245
Washington (state), 125
Washington (town), 135
Washington University, 202
Webster Groves, 25
Wells, Robert William, 283
Western Hemisphere, 22
Western Sanitary Commission, 170
Weston, 107
Westphalia, 135, 136
Westport, Battle of, 169
Westport Landing, 107, 124, 125
Wetmore, Alphonso, 270
Wheatland, 126
Whiteman, George, 226
Whiteman Air Force Base, 226, 231
White River, 107
Wilder, Laura Ingalls, 271, 272–73, 274
Wilson, Woodrow, 208
Wilson's Creek, Battle of, 163, 166, 167, 170, 181
Winona, 192
Wisconsin, 273
Wittenberg, 135
Women
    in French Missouri, ix, 62
    on the frontier, 92, 94, 96
    Native American, 8, 11–12, 59
    the vote for, 142, 184, 185, 214–15
    in the Civil War, 170–71
    in World War I, 208
    in the 1920s, 214–15
    in World War II, 228
    after World War II, 238
Woodland Indians, 5
Woods, Harriet, 234
World War I, 207
    America in, 208
    end of, 212
    Missourians and, 208–12

World War II
   American involvement in, 225–26
   end of, 231
   Missourians and, 226–31
   reasons for, 225–26
Worlds of Fun (Kansas City), 263

Wright, Harold Bell, 271
Wyaconda, 14

York (African-American slave), 77
Young, Hiram, 156
Younger, Cole, 170